L.A. DECK
Daniel Newman

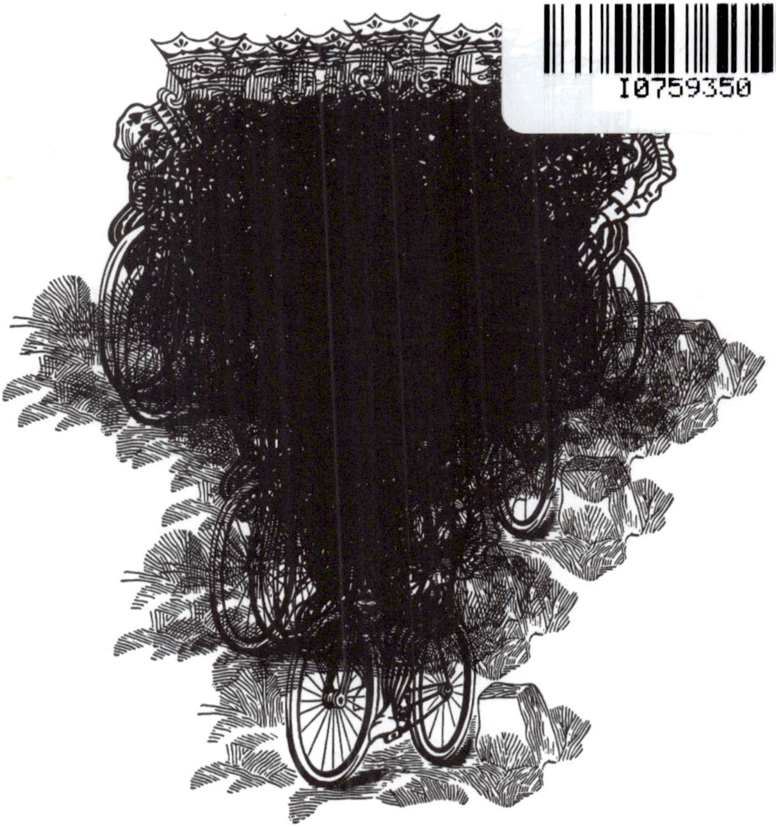

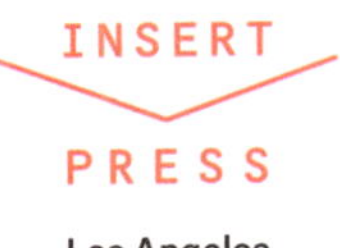

L.A. DECK
©Daniel Newman, 2022

Insert Press

ISBN: 978-1-947322-04-2
Library of Congress Control Number: 2022944741

Design and Layout by Mathew Timmons.
Inside front cover by Matt Normand.

L.A. Deck documents a multi-year project in which the artist Daniel Newman collected an entire deck of playing cards one-by-one over an extended period of time, on the streets and in the gutters of Los Angeles.

L.A. Deck was exhibited in the show 52 PICKUP: Daniel Newman at General Projects, Los Angeles. Newman's solo show opened on Leap Day, Saturday, February 29th, 2020 and ran until mid March 2020 when the statewide "stay at home" order was issued in the state of California.

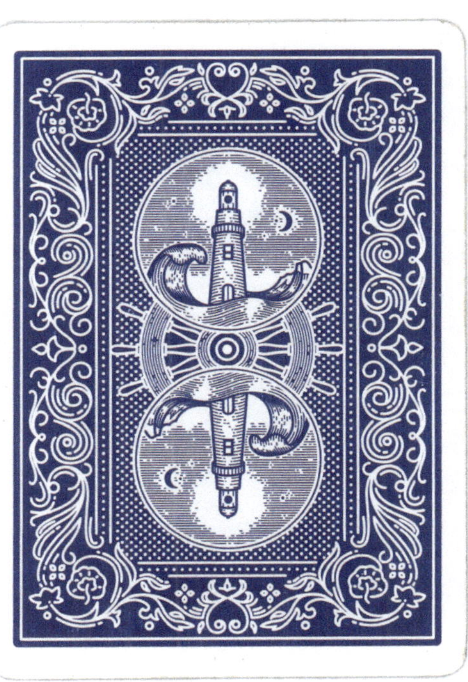

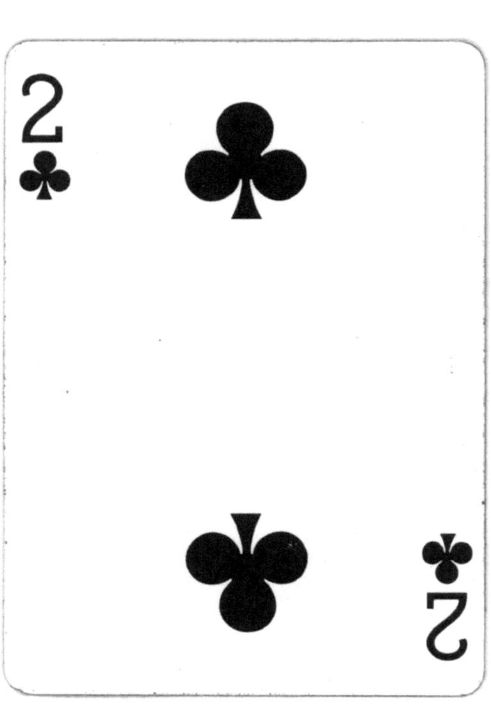

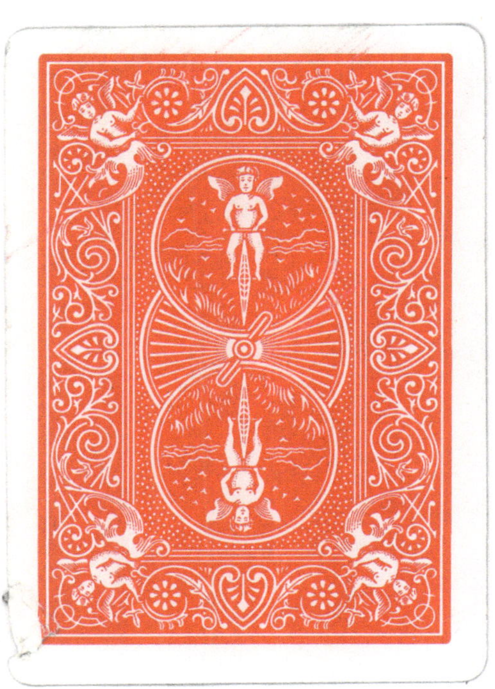

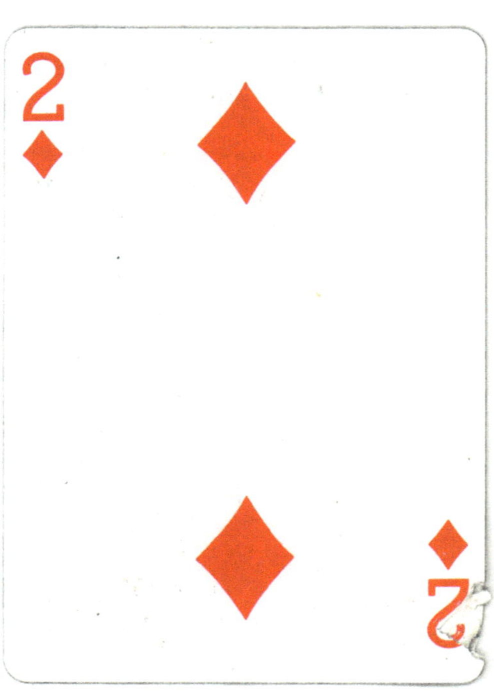

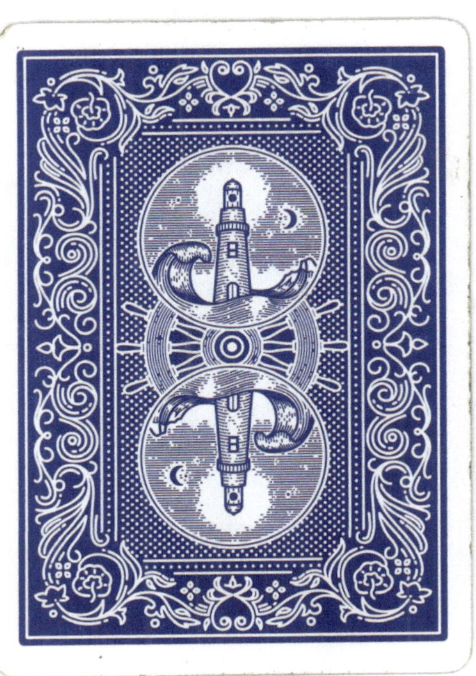

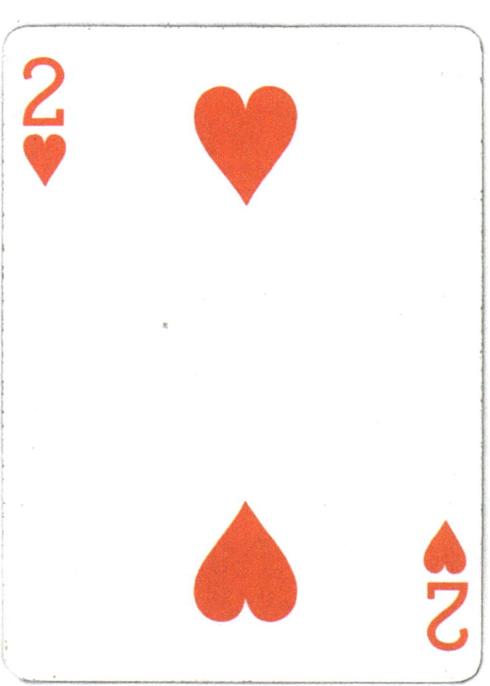

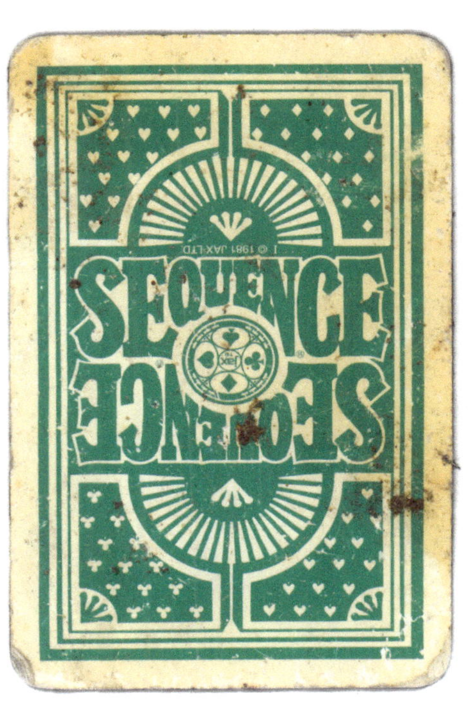

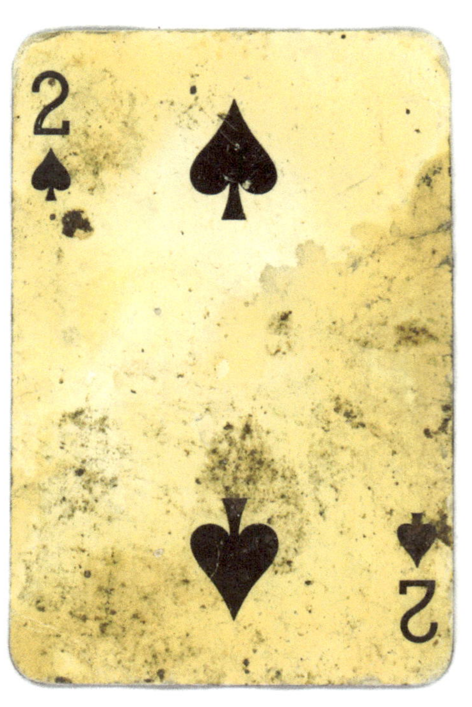

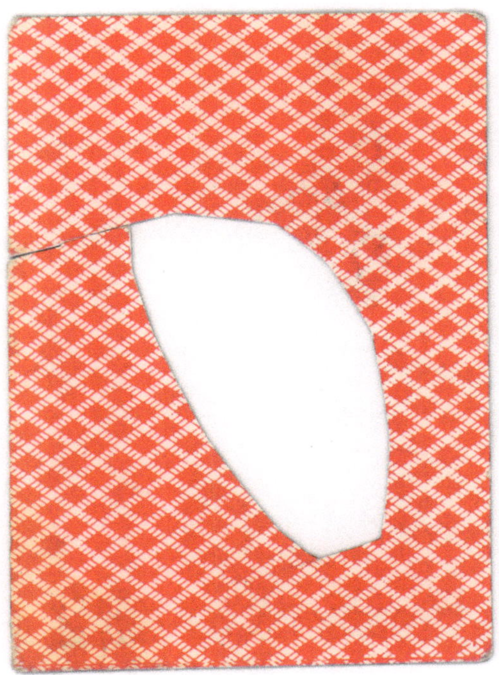

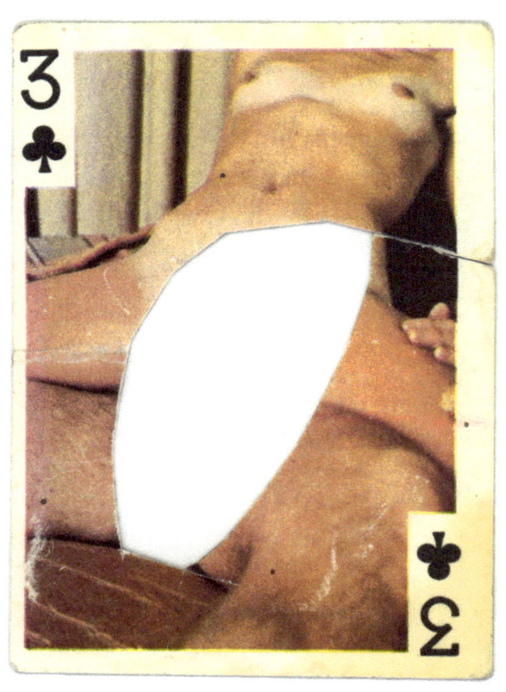

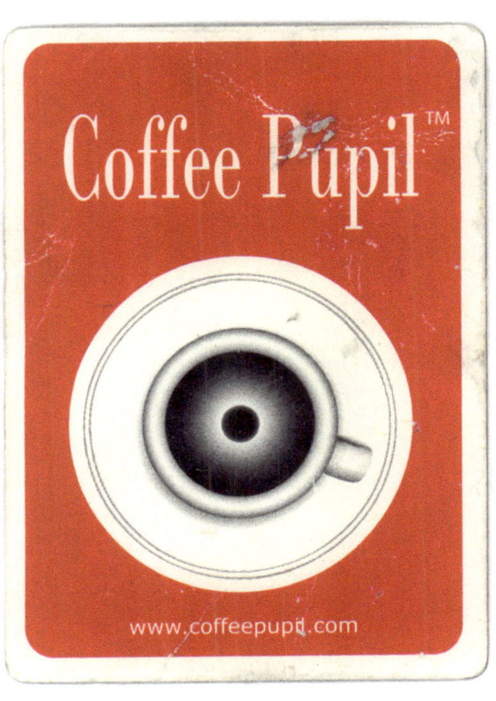

Coffee Pupil™
www.coffeepupil.com

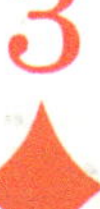

3 ♦

Karnataka, Kerala and
Tamil Nadu produce most
of which country's coffee?

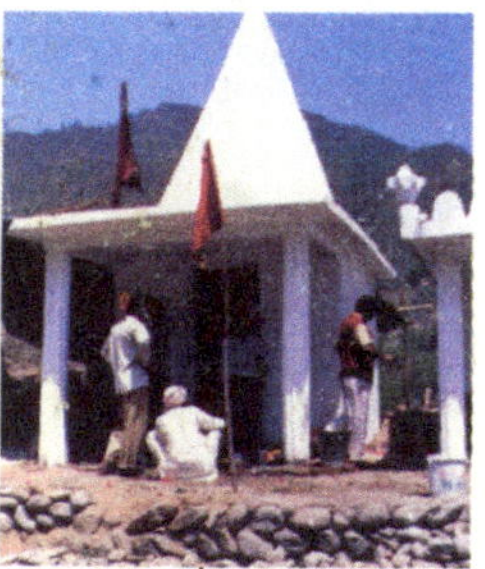

India (produced 4.6M bags
in 2003).[4] These regions are
located in the Western Ghat
mountains in the south.

Find:
luck
WORKBOOKstock

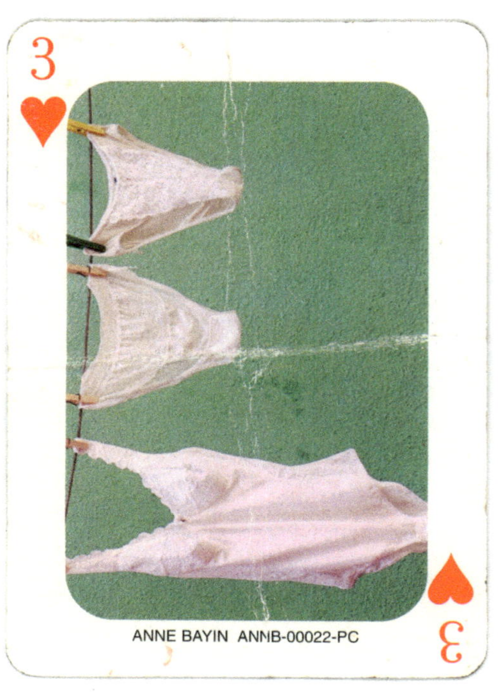
3
ANNE BAYIN ANNB-00022-PC
3

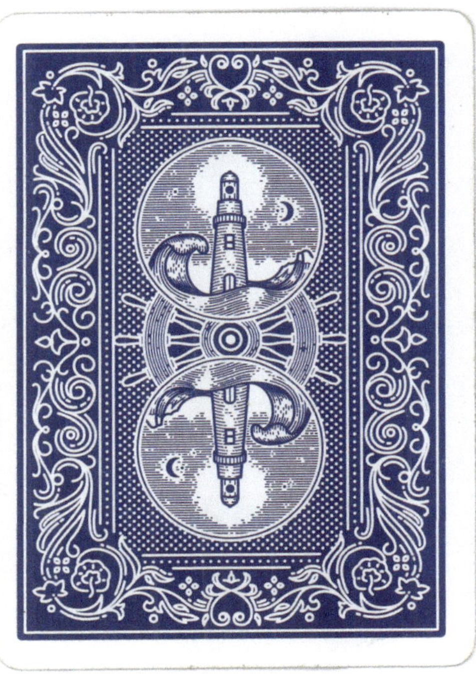

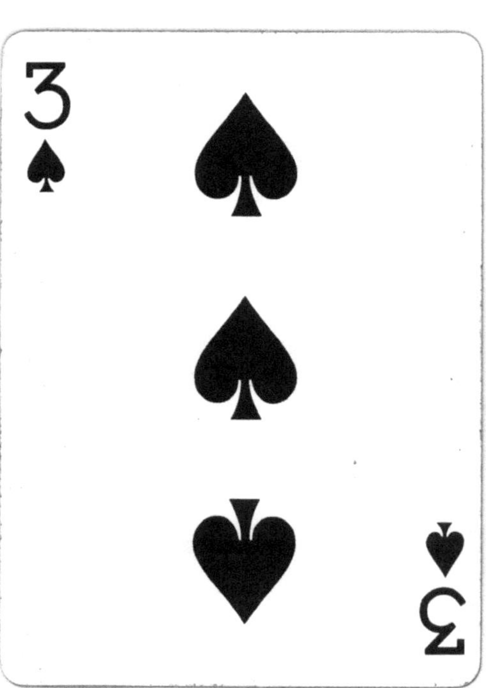

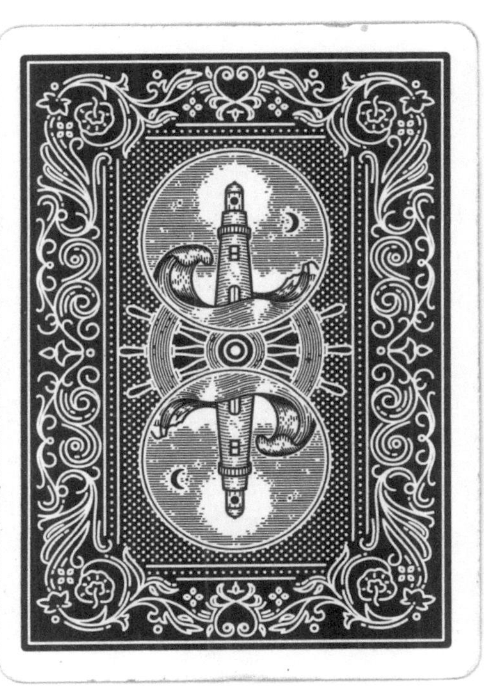

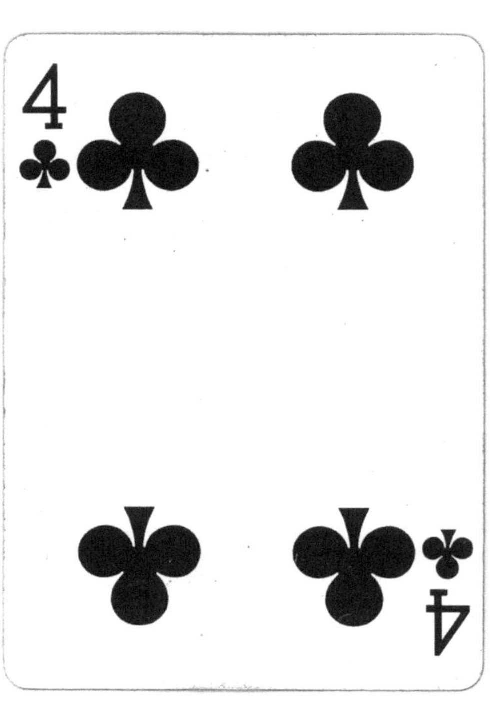

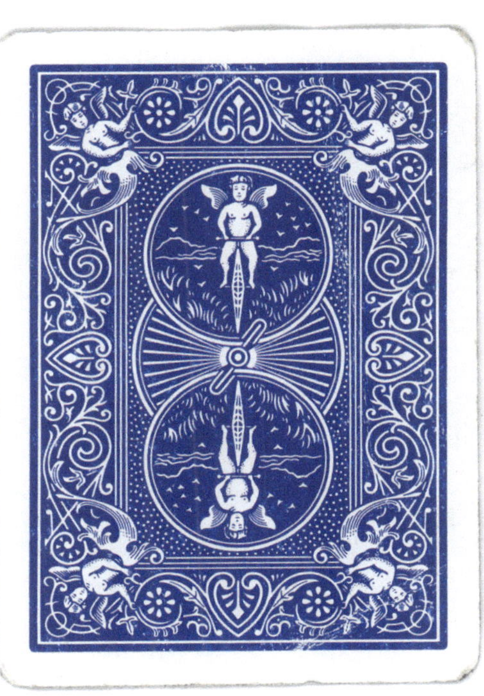

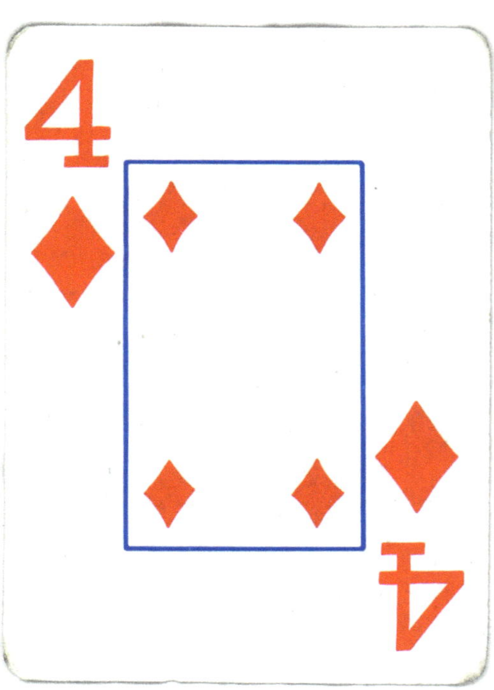

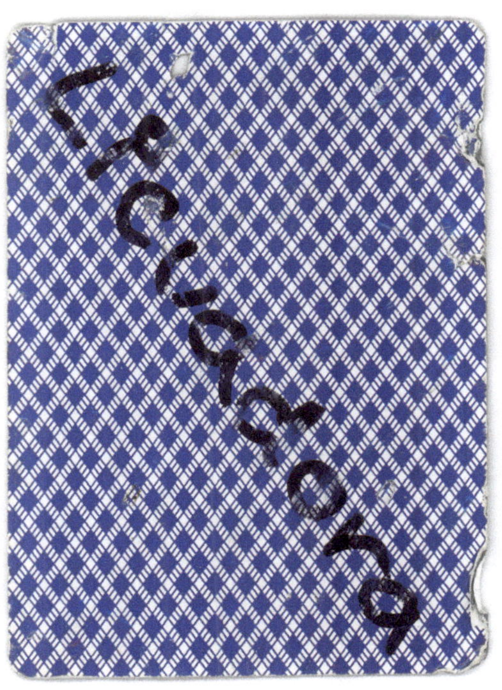
Crevadora

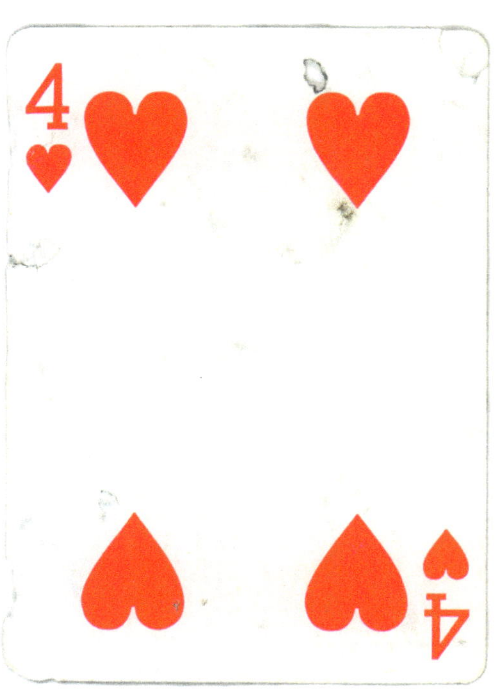

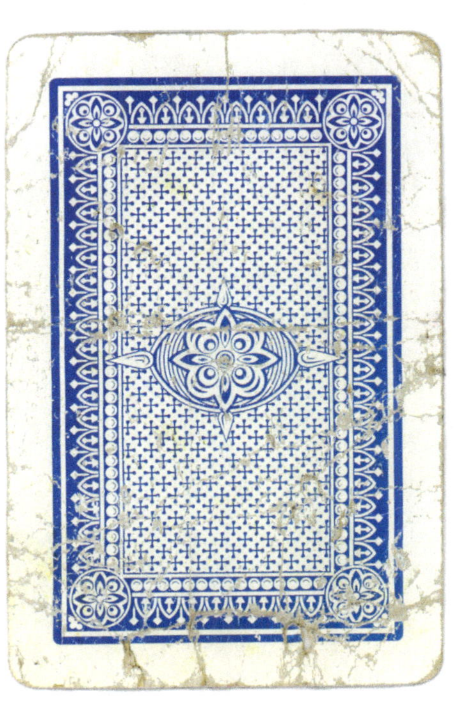

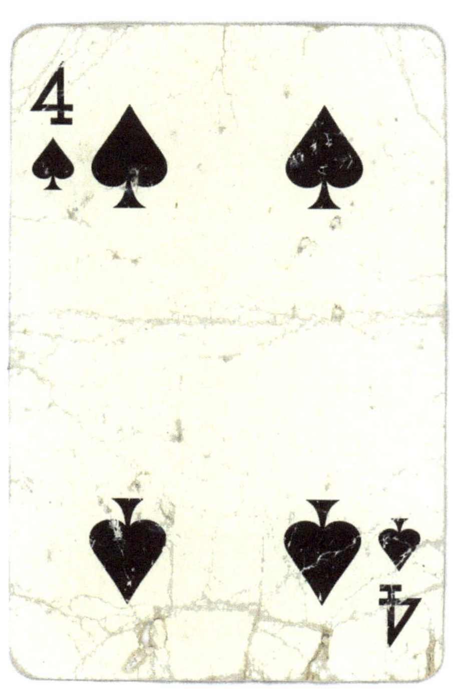

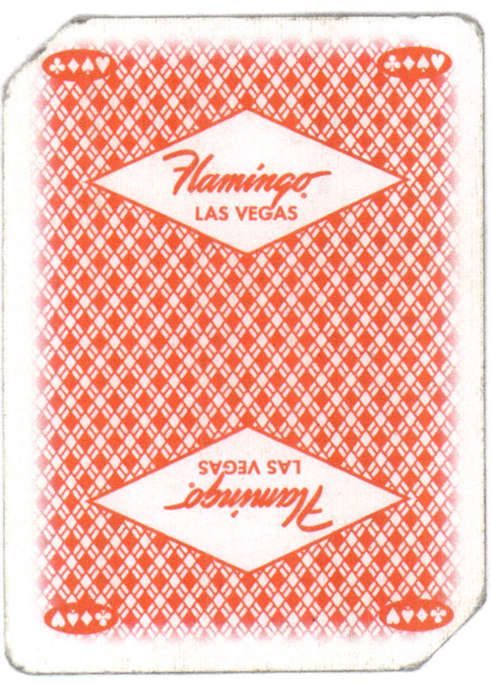

Flamingo
LAS VEGAS

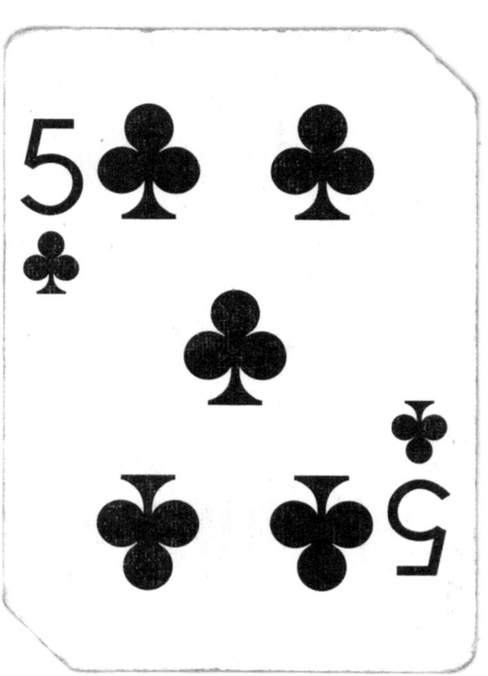

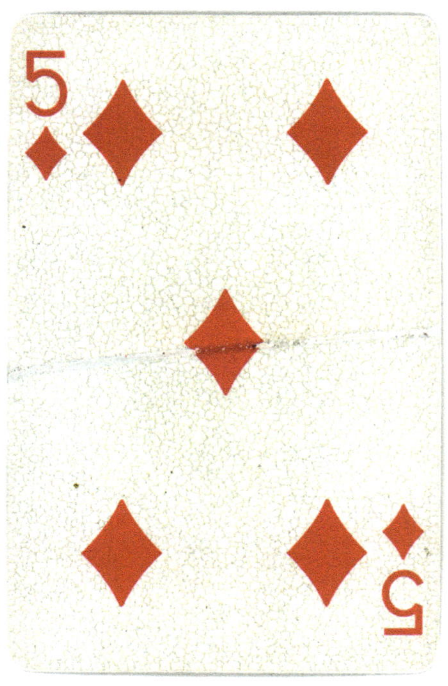

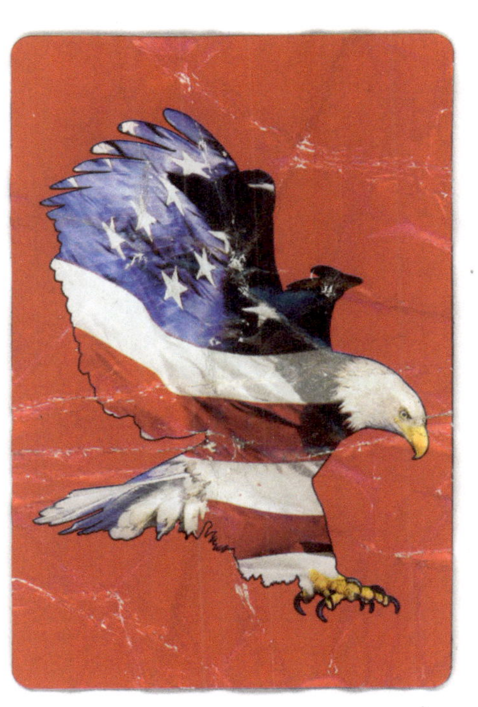

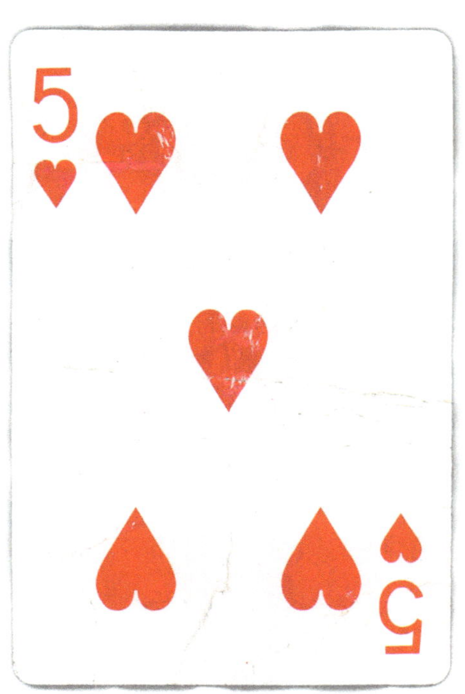

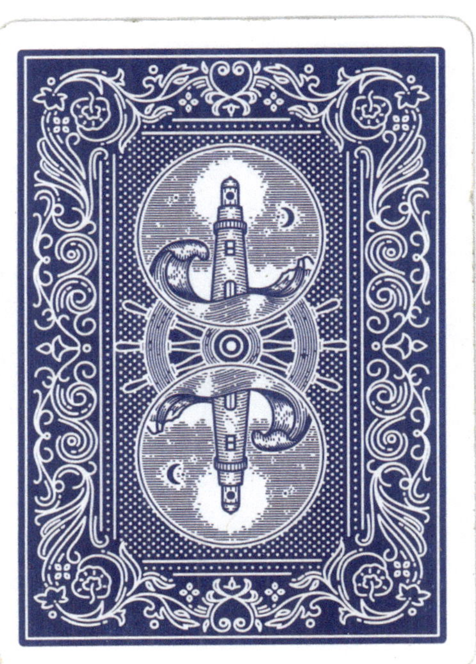

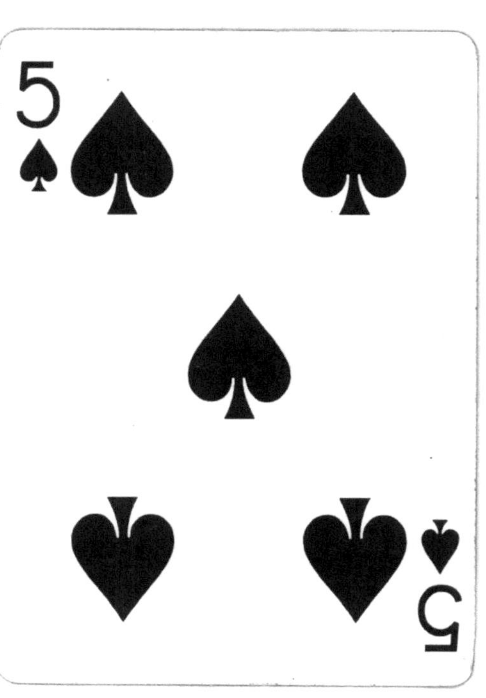

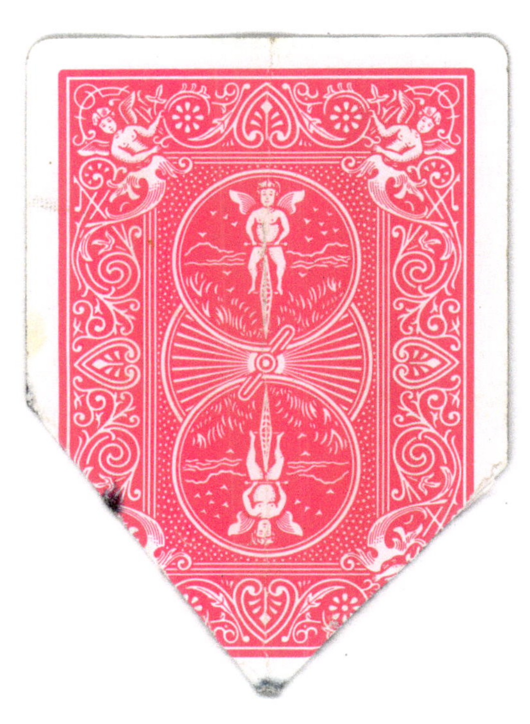

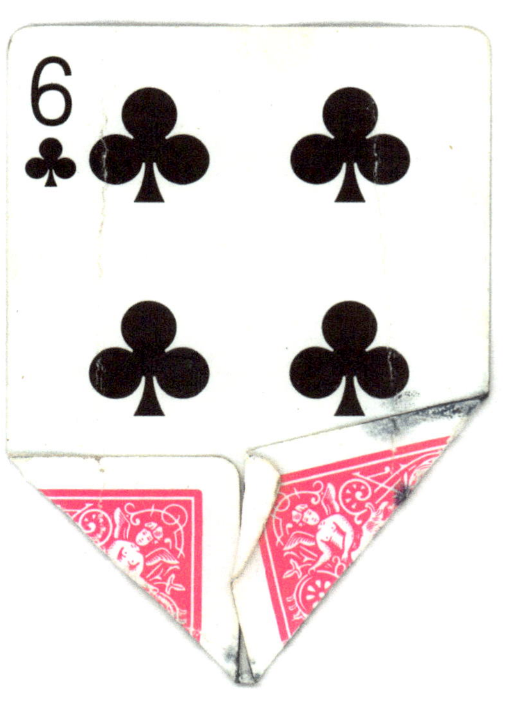

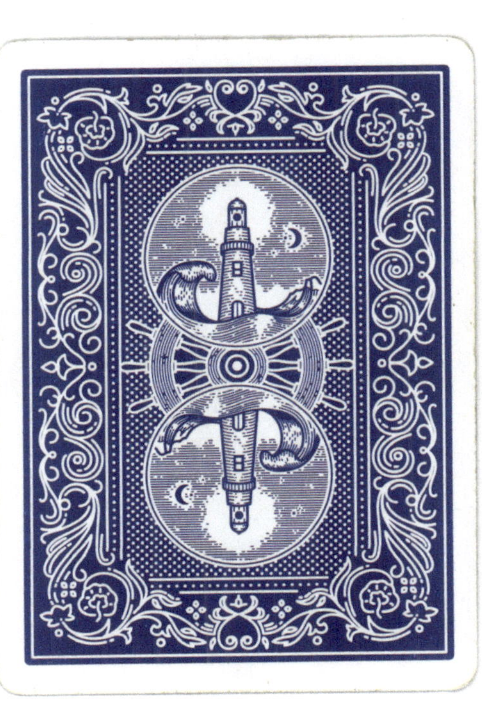

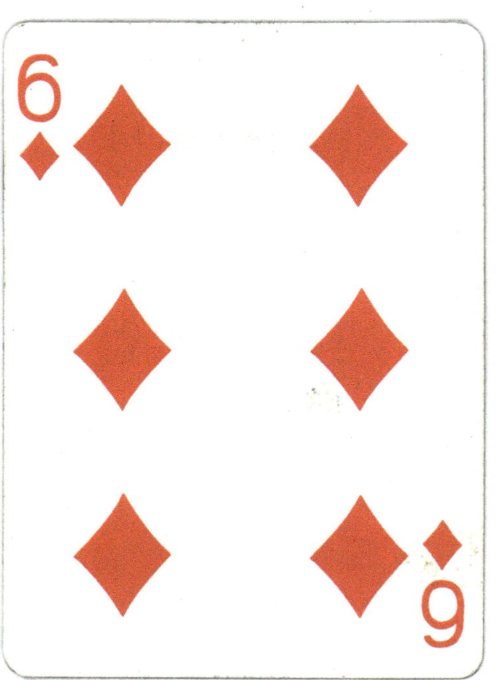

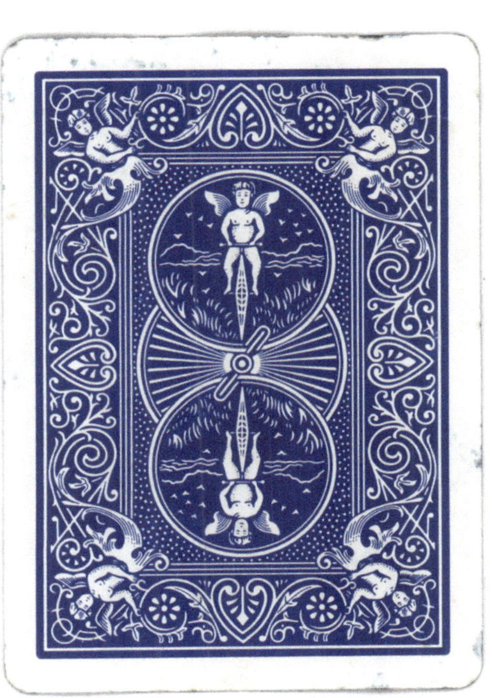

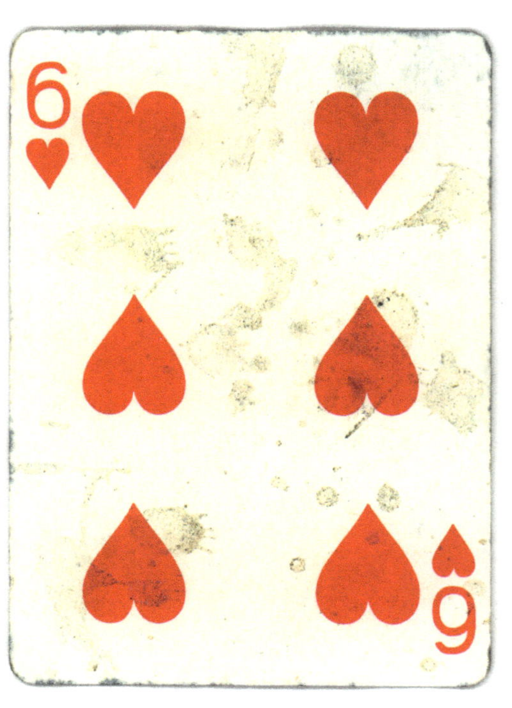

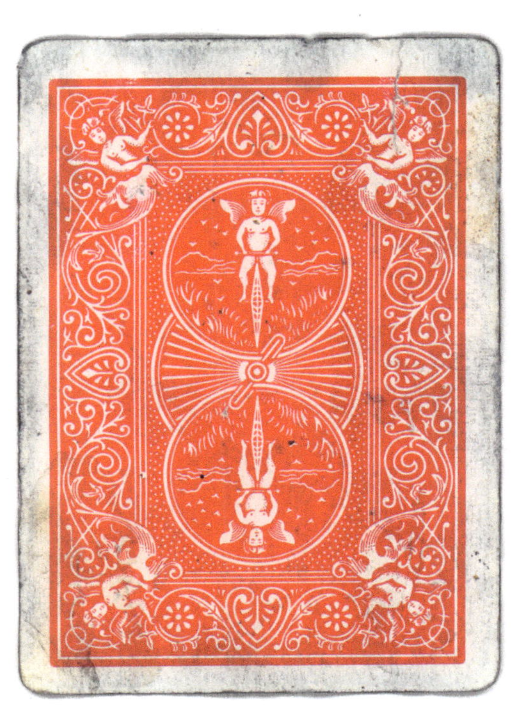

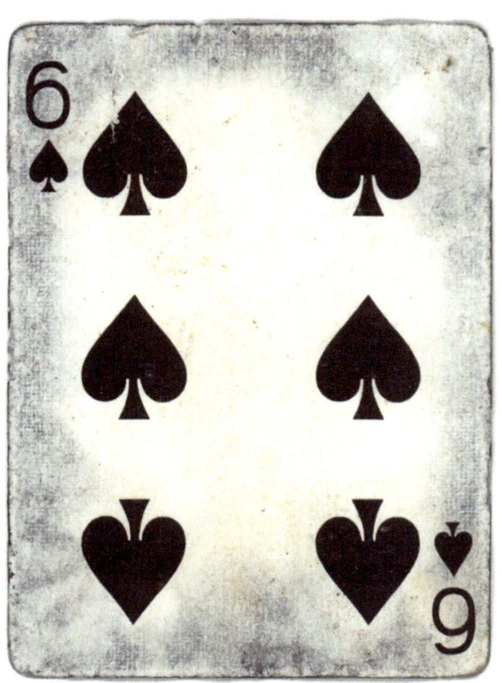

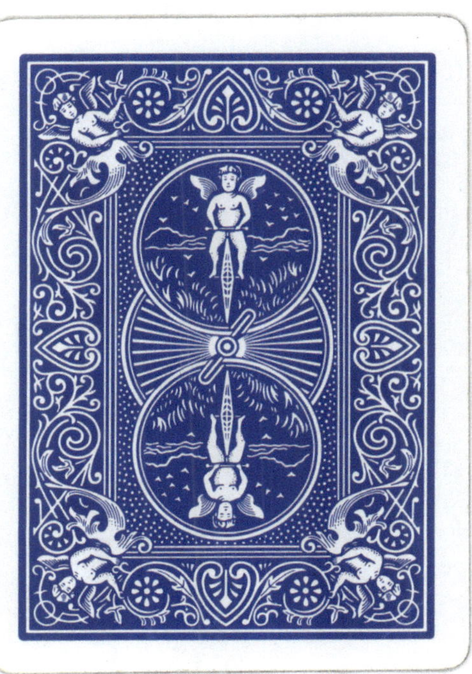

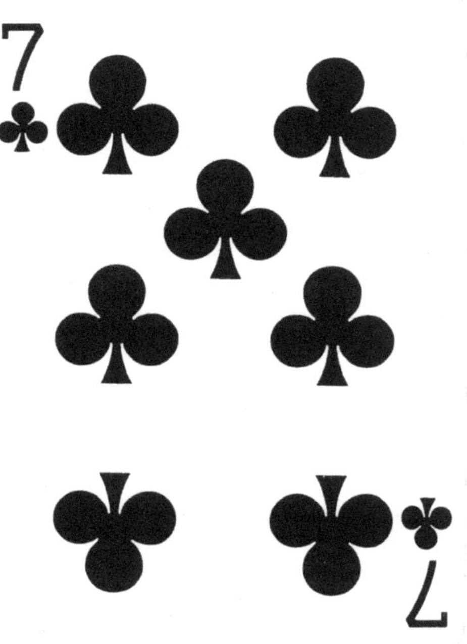

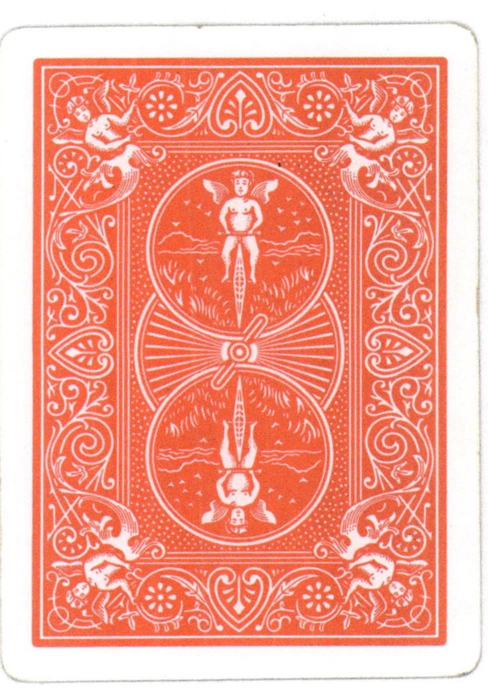

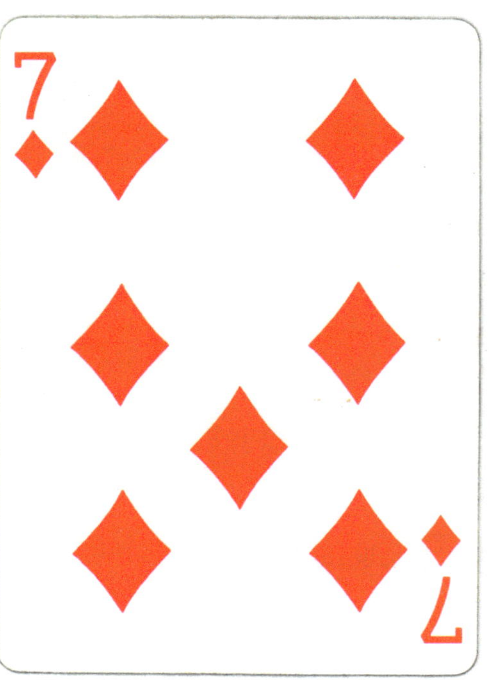

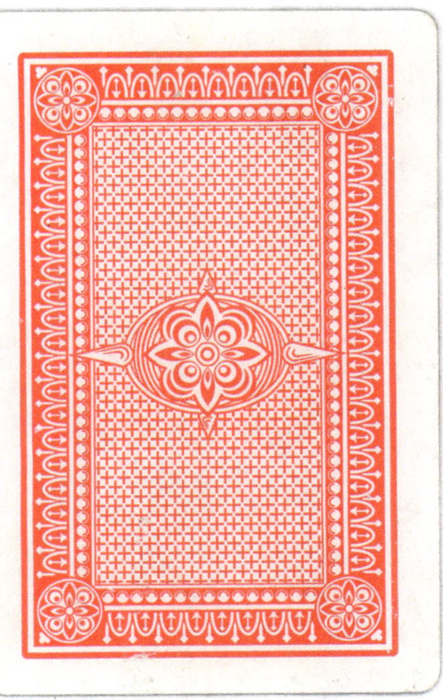

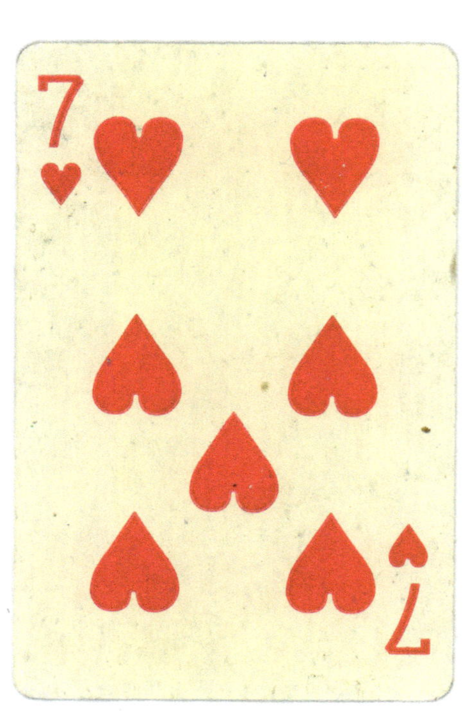

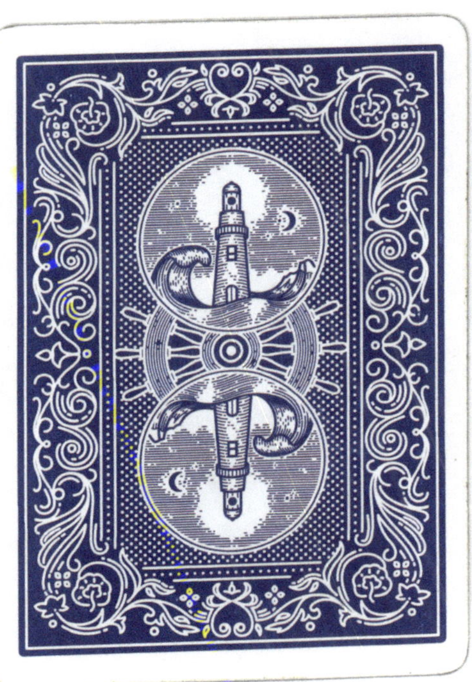

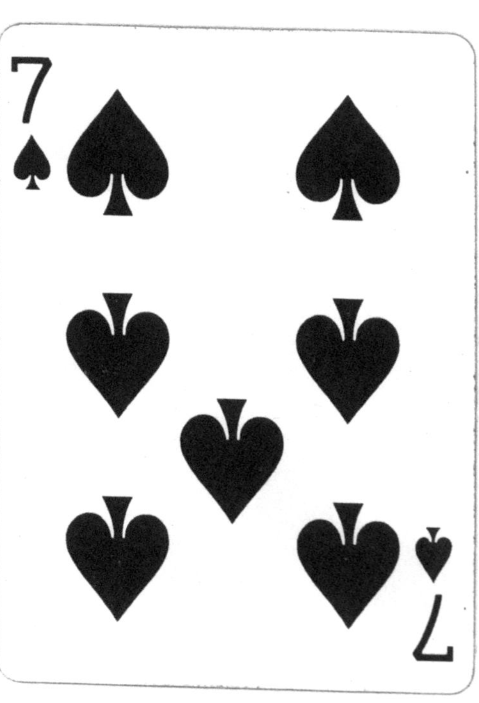

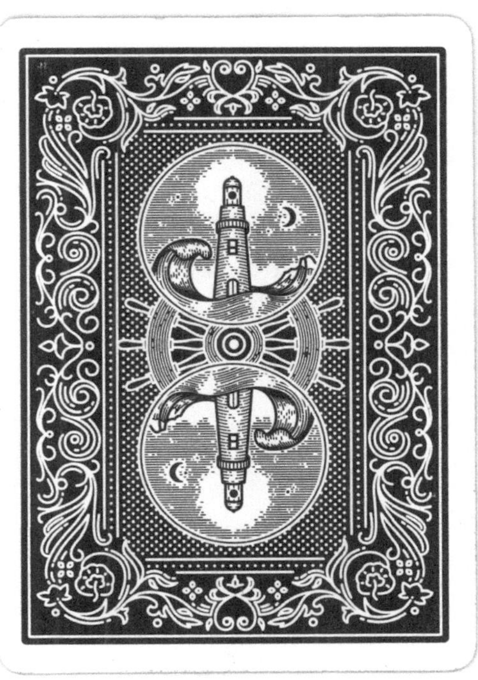

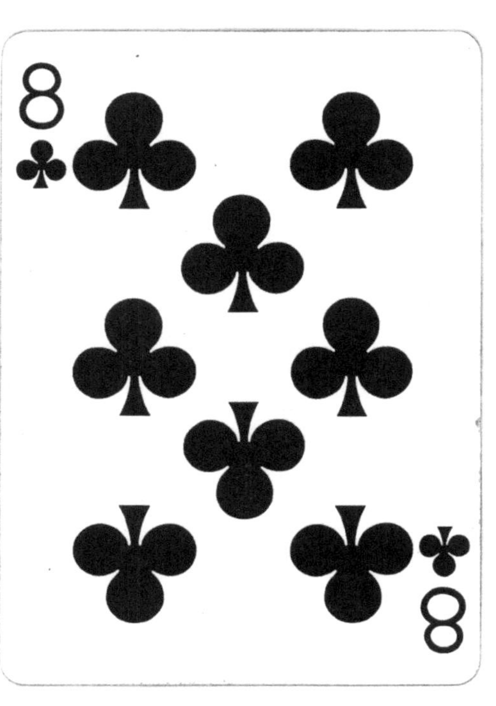

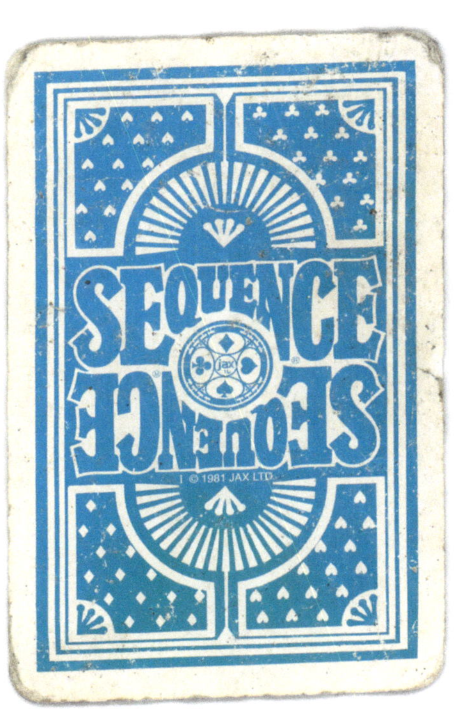

SEQUENCE
SEQUENCE
I © 1981 JAX LTD.

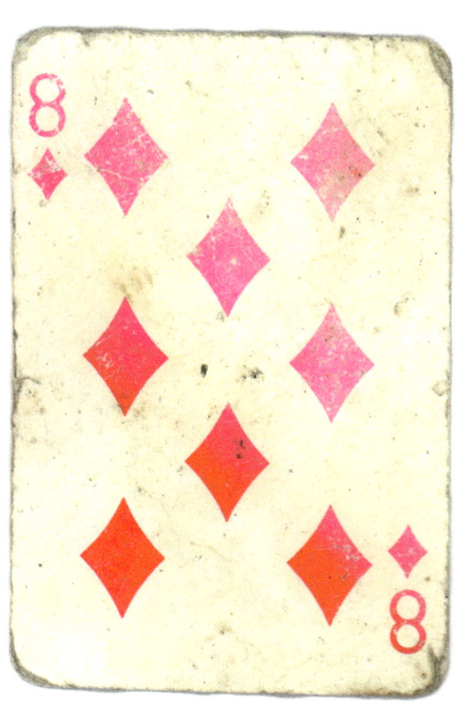

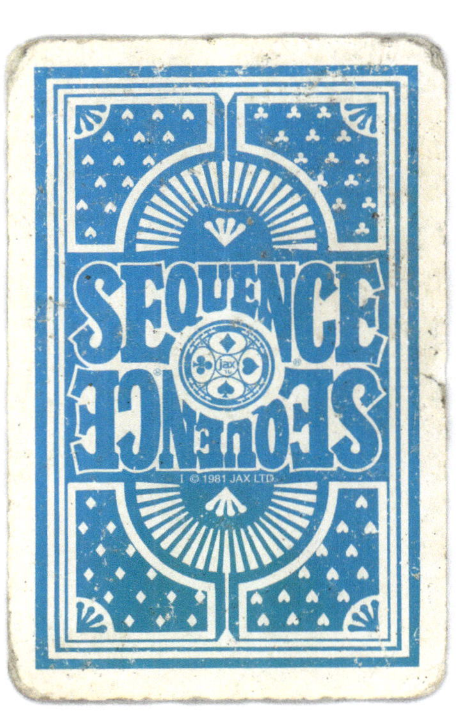

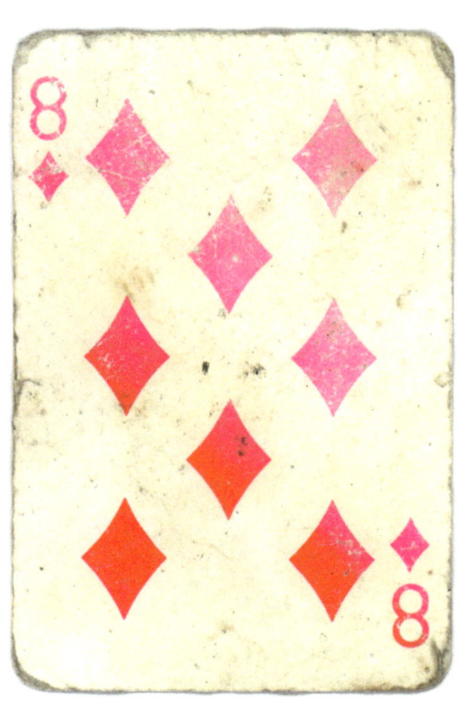

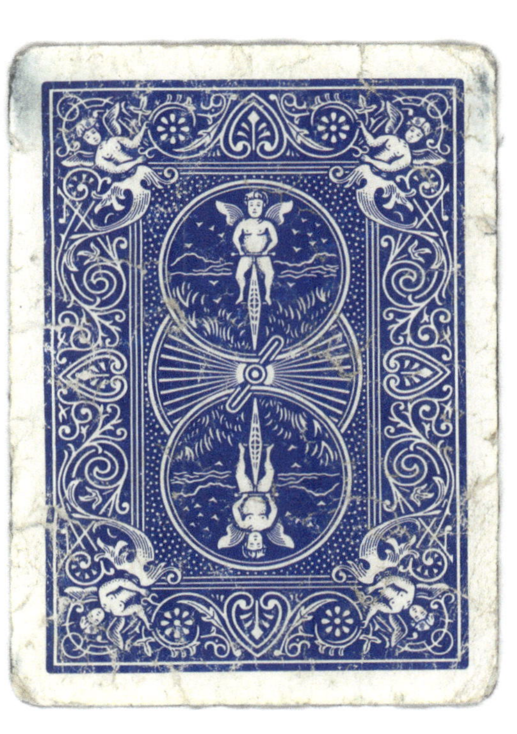

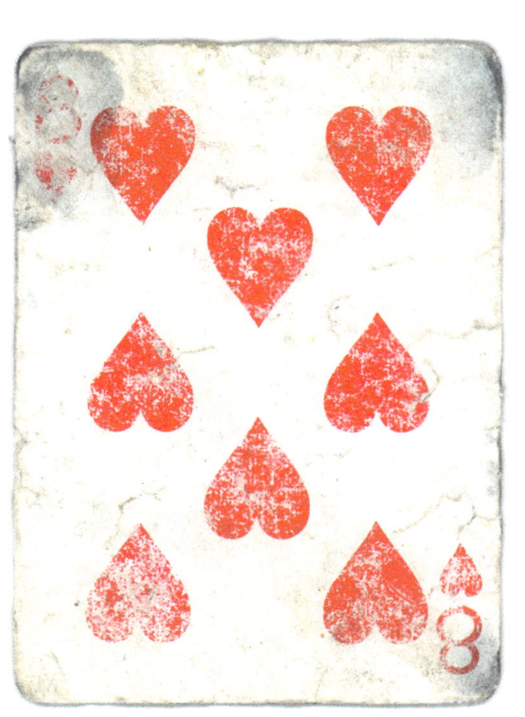

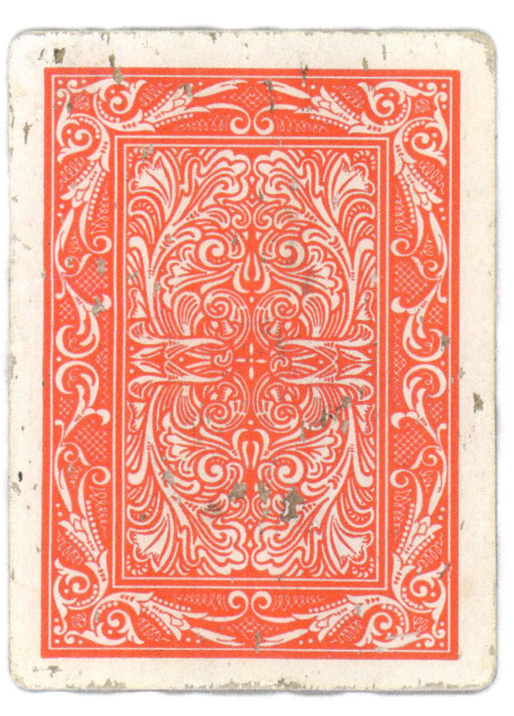

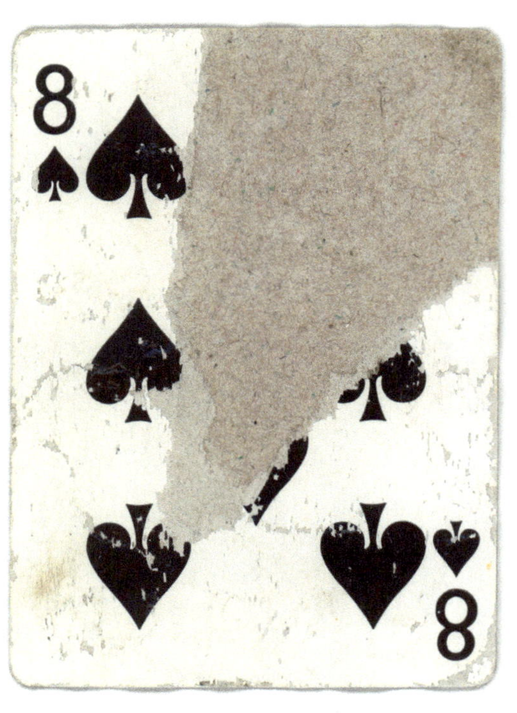

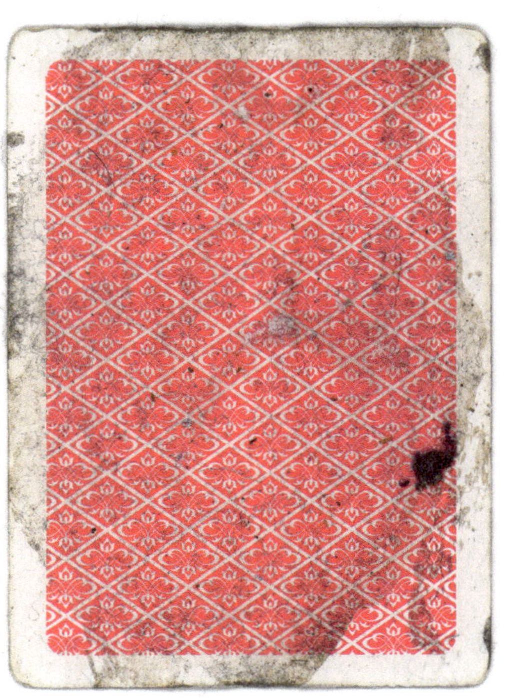

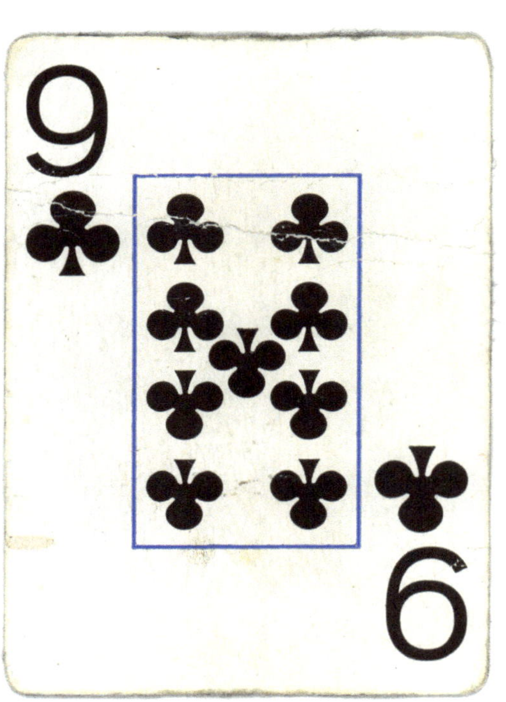

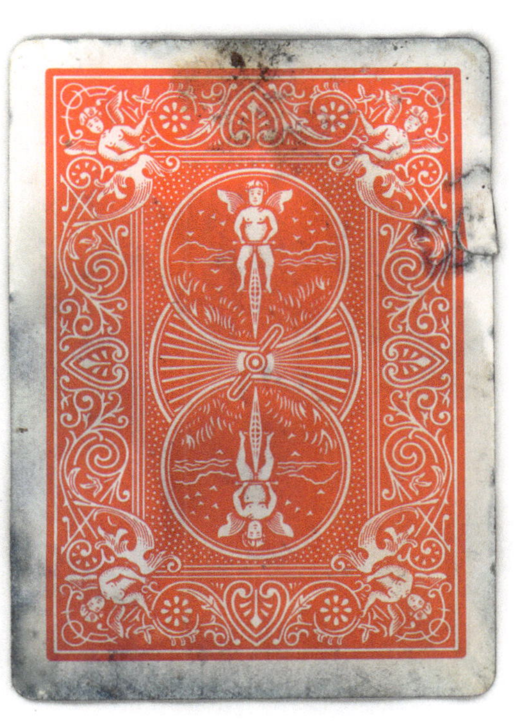

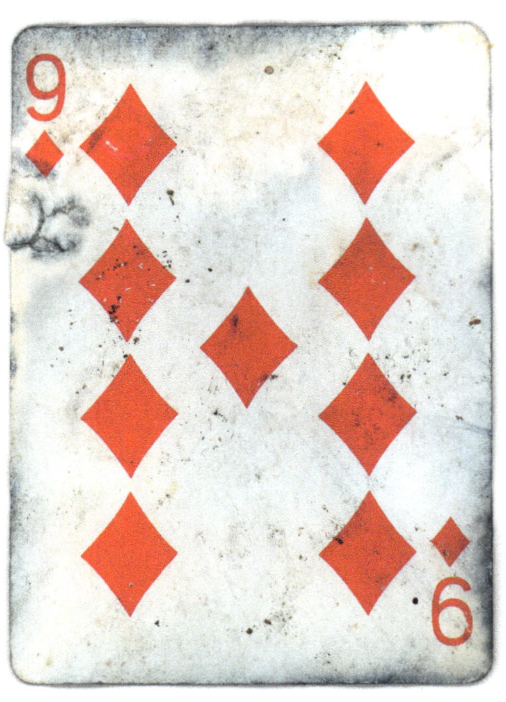

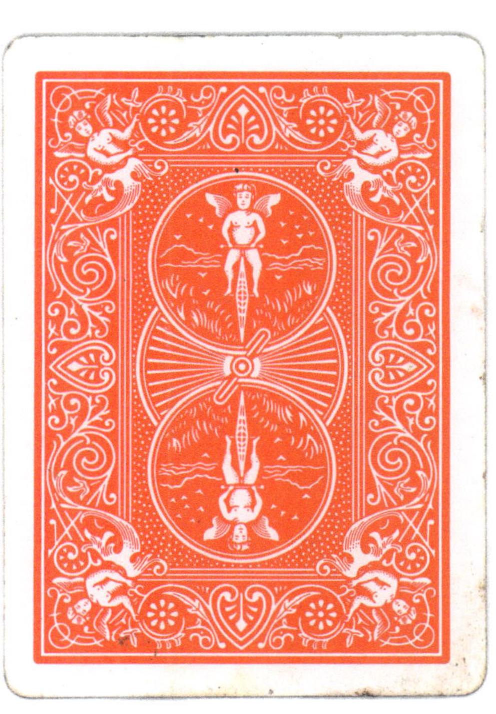

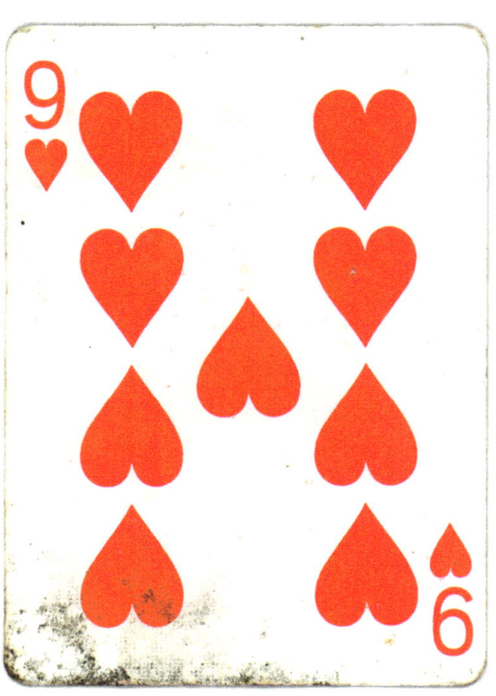

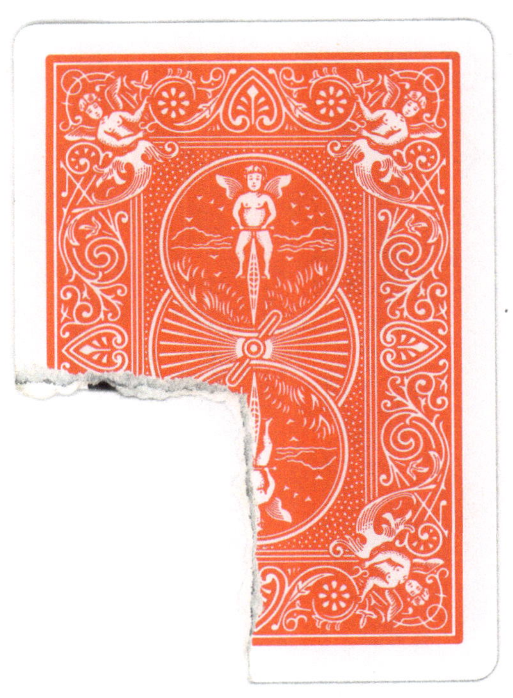

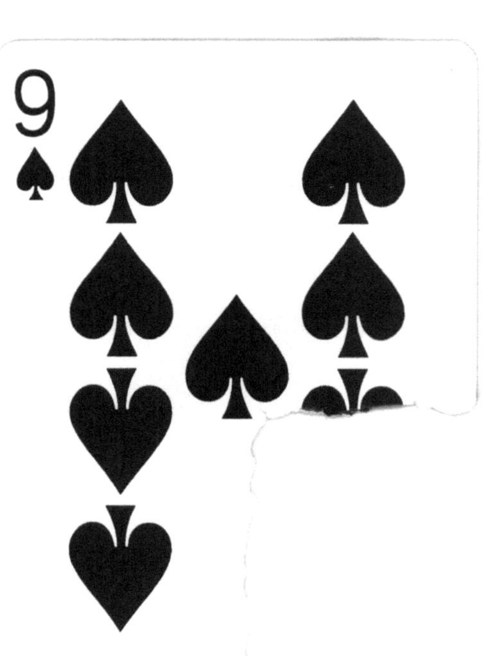

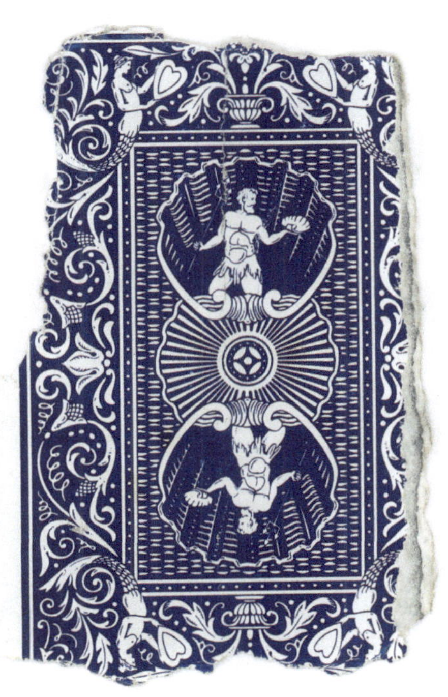

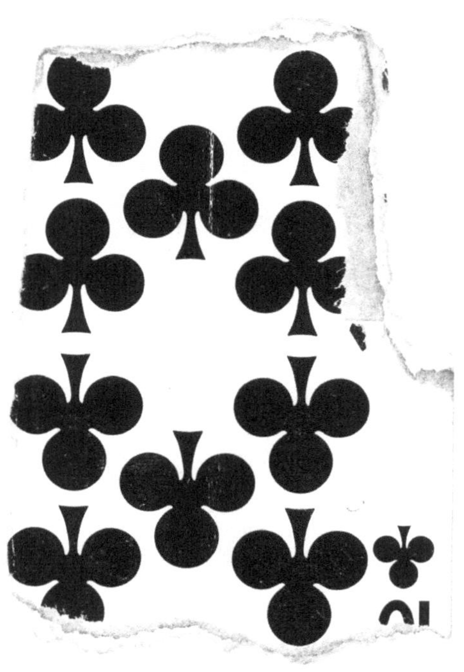

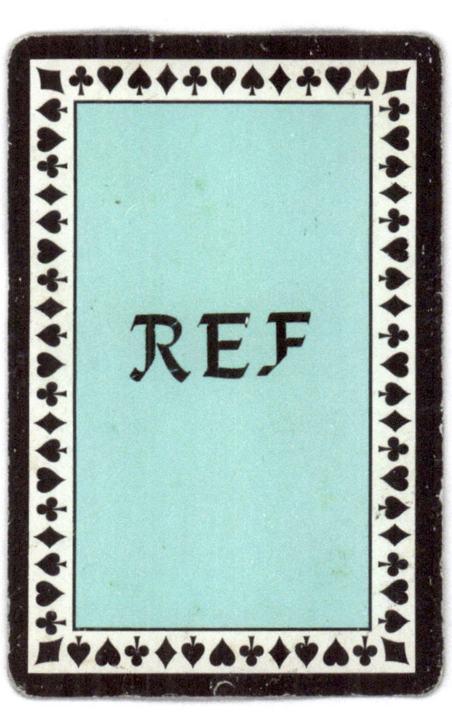
REF

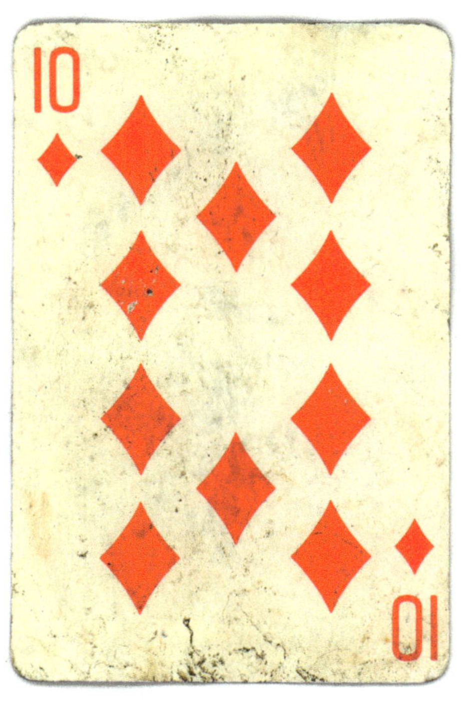

Find:
luck
WORKBOOKstock

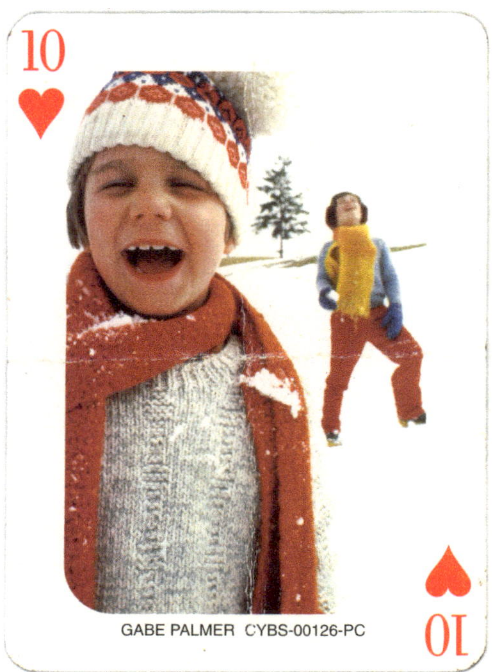

10
GABE PALMER CYBS-00126-PC
10

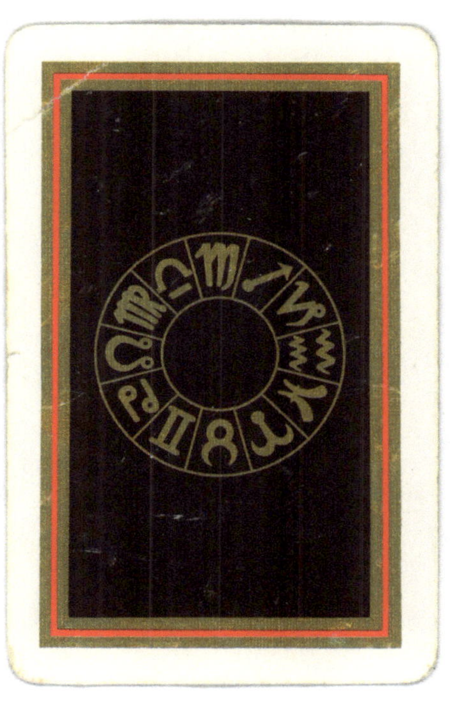

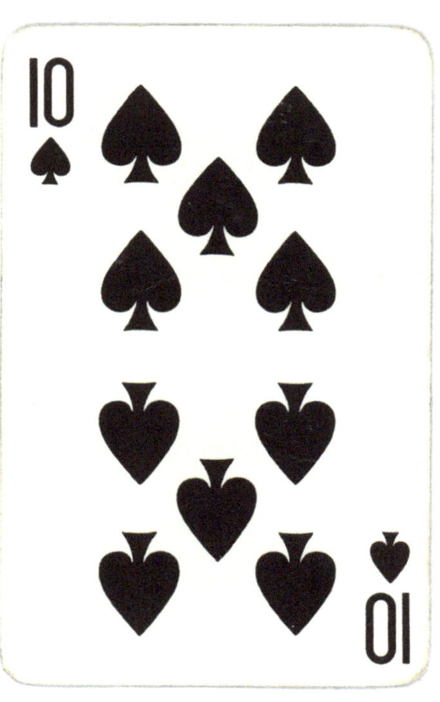

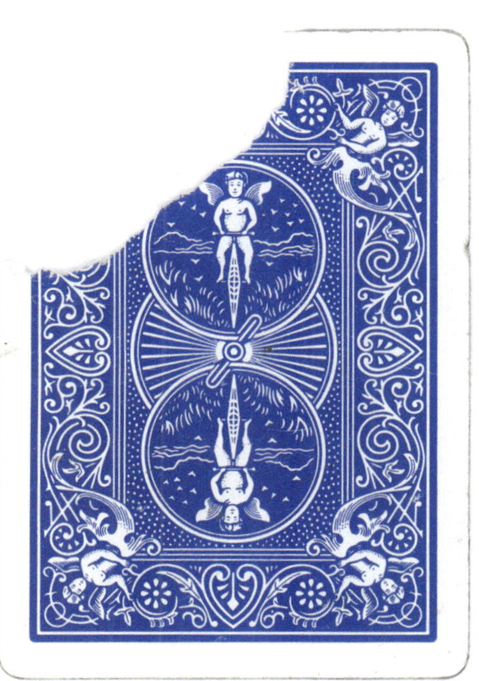

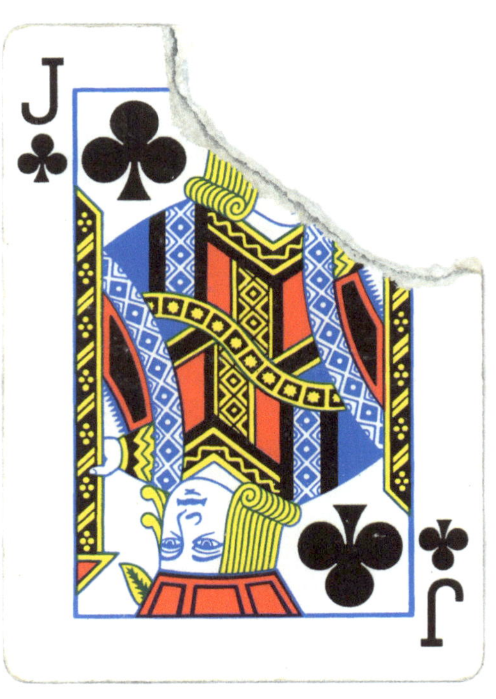

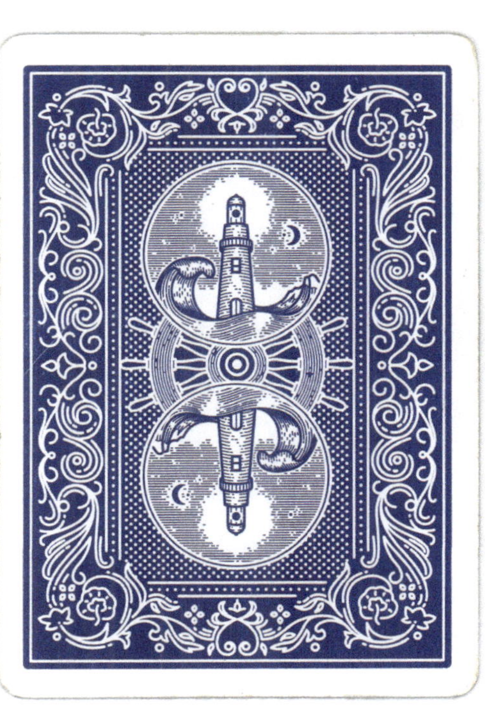

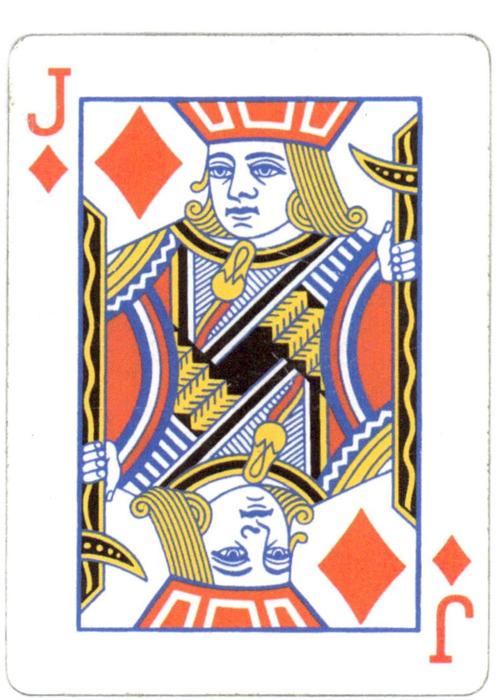

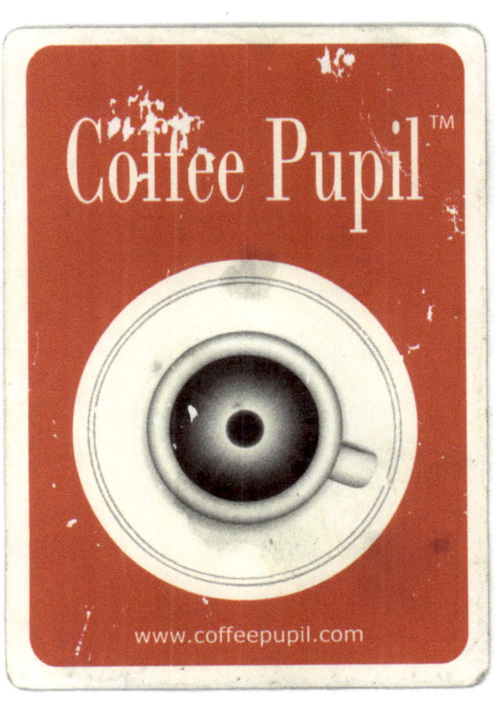

Coffee Pupil™
www.coffeepupil.com

J ♥

What is a portafilter?

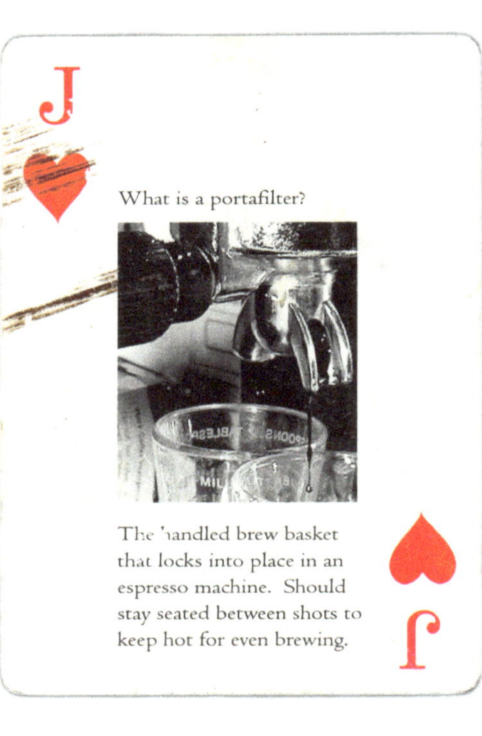

The handled brew basket that locks into place in an espresso machine. Should stay seated between shots to keep hot for even brewing.

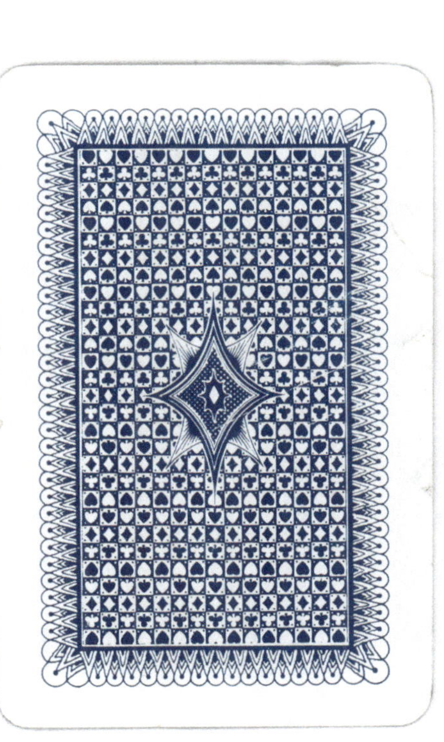

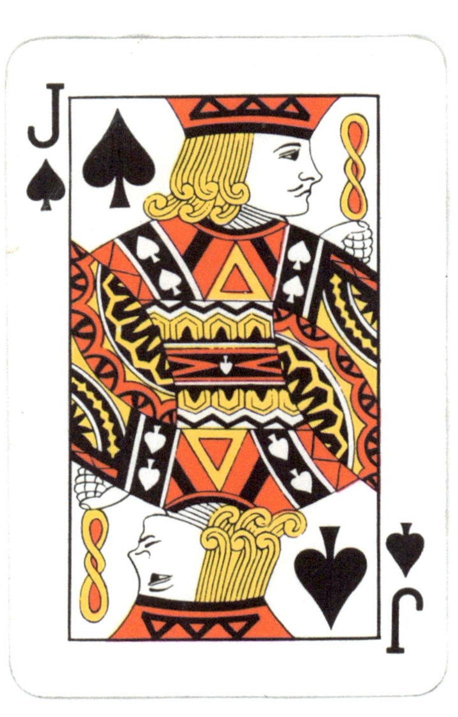

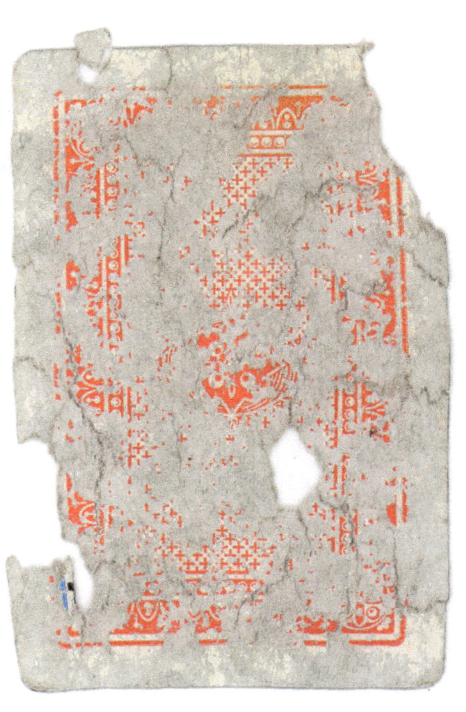

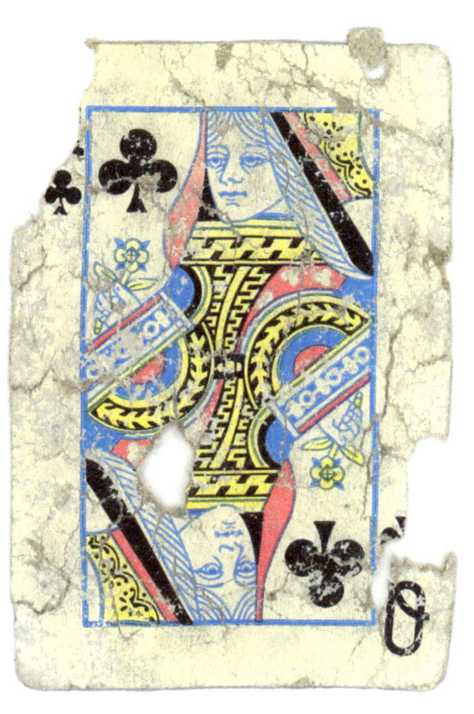

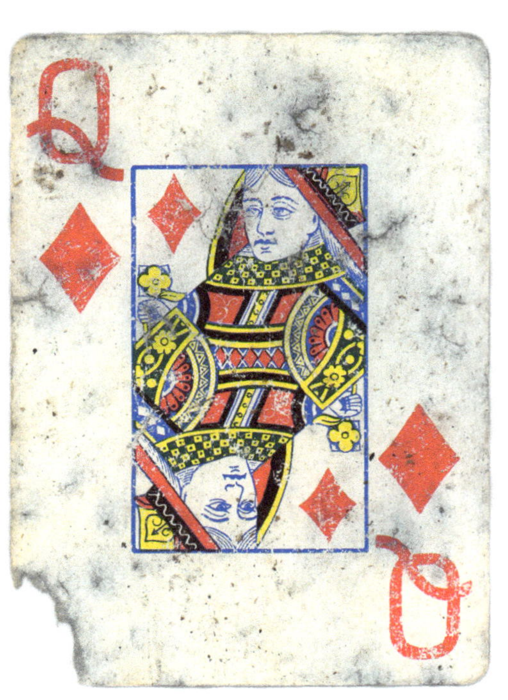

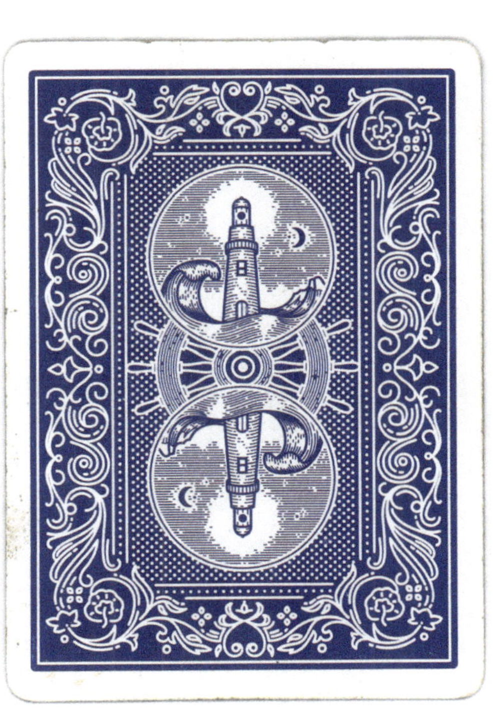

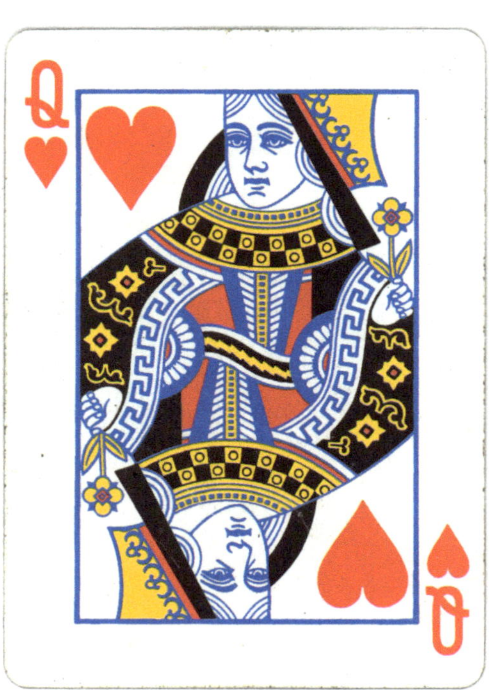

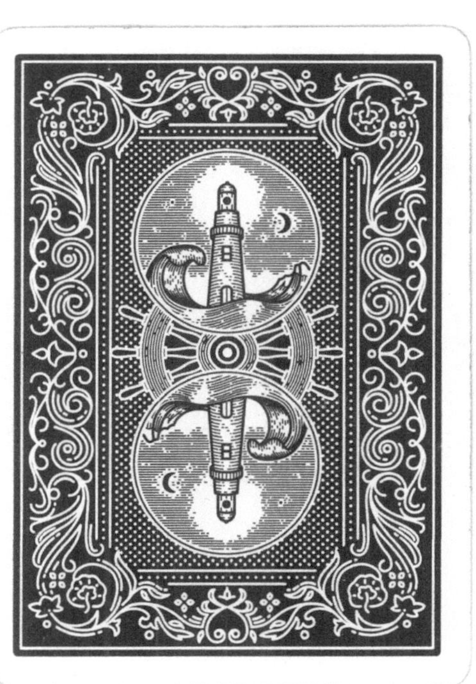

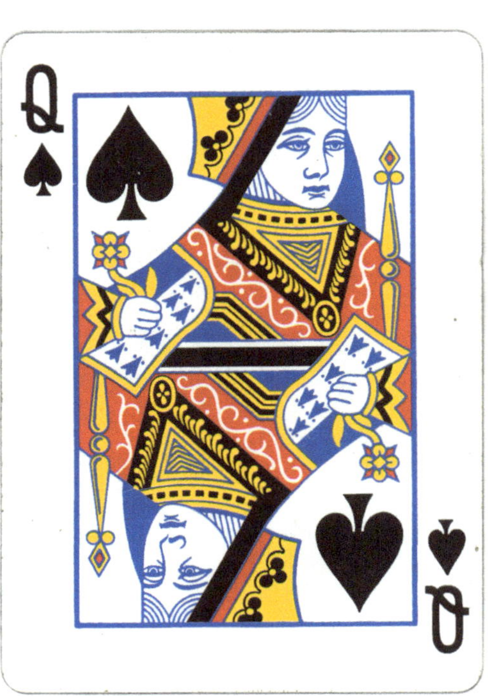

Find:
luck
WORKBOOKstock

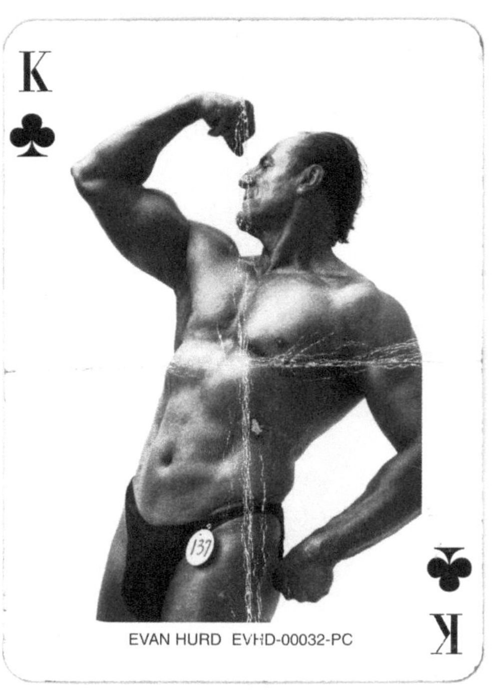
K
137
EVAN HURD EVHD-00032-PC

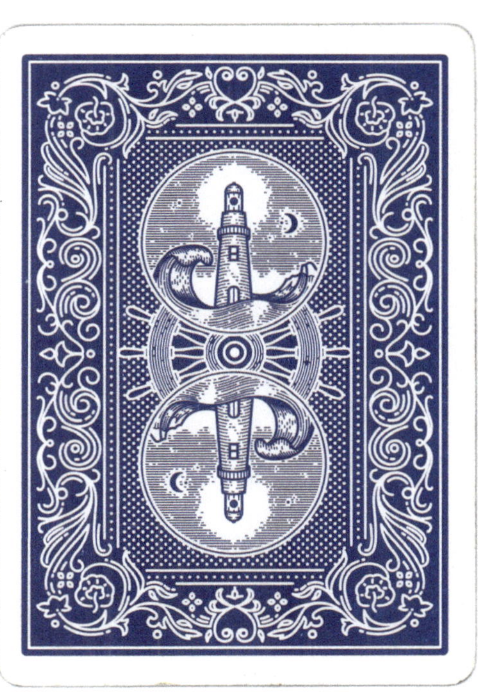

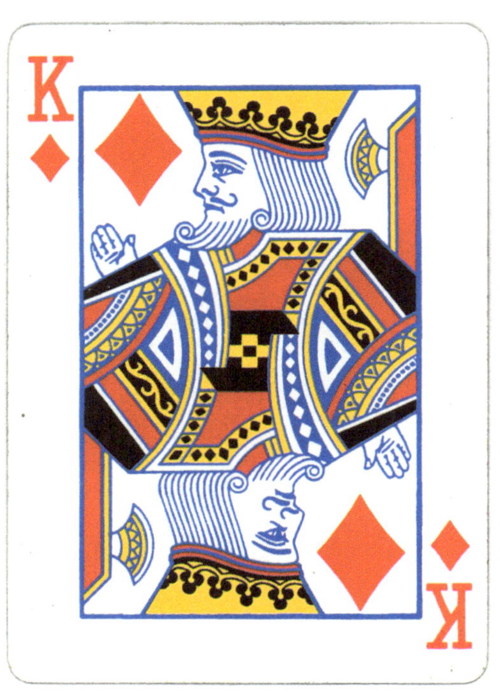

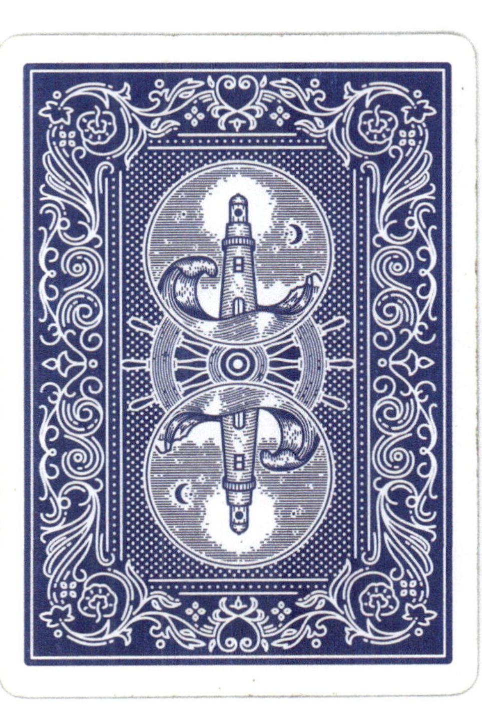

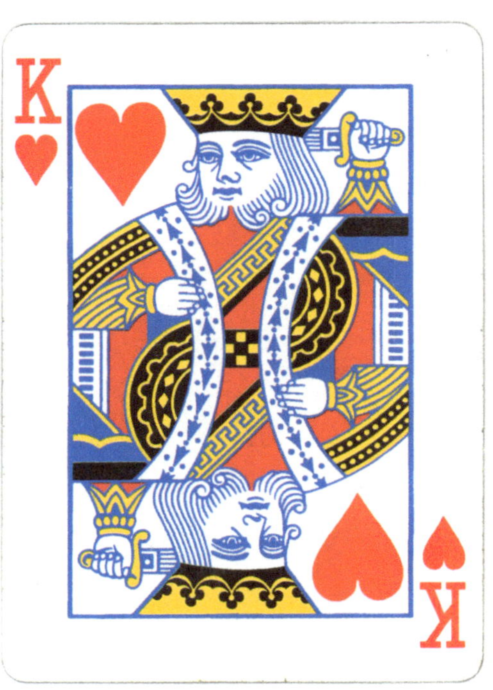

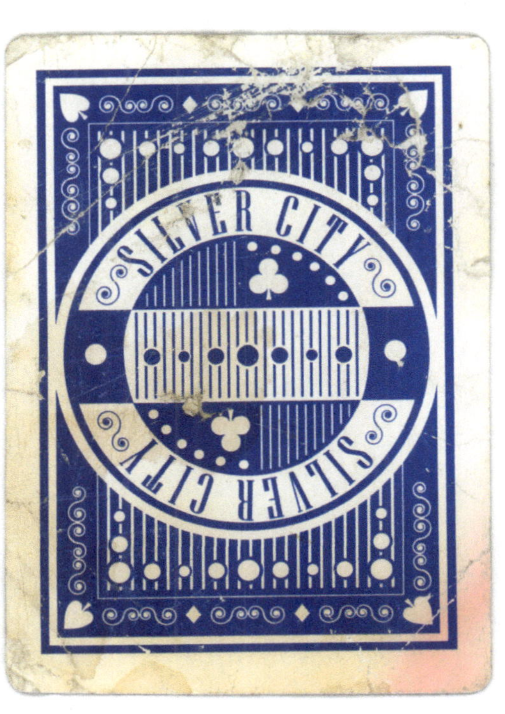

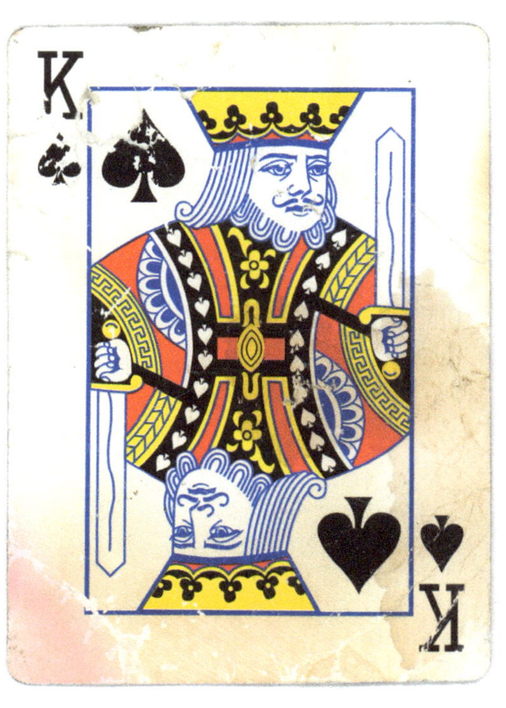

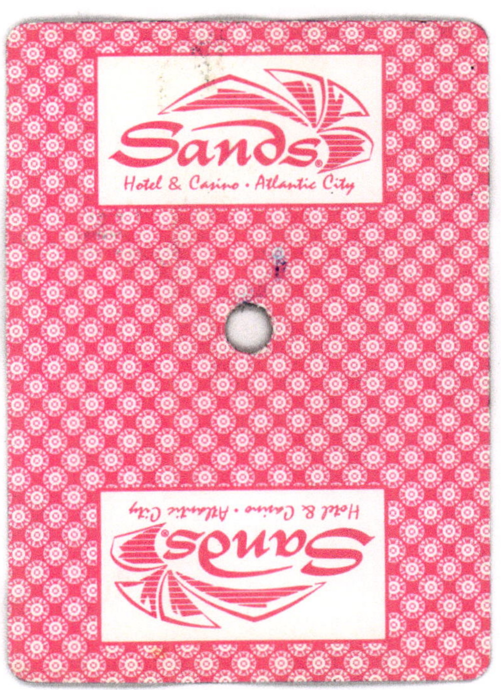

Sands.
Hotel & Casino · Atlantic City
Sands.
Hotel & Casino · Atlantic City

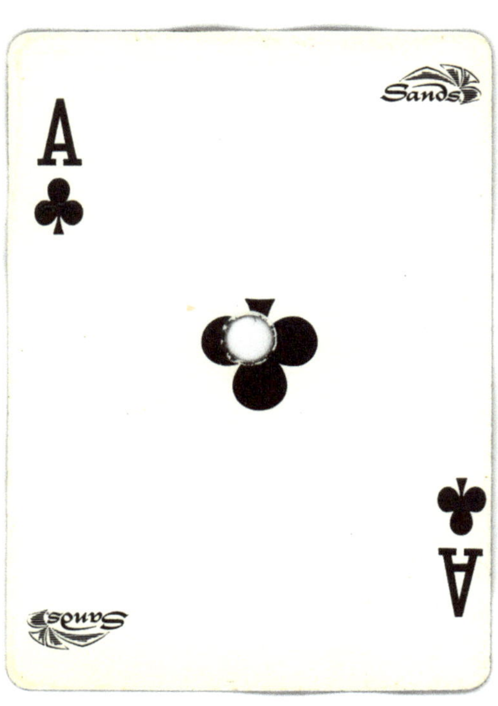

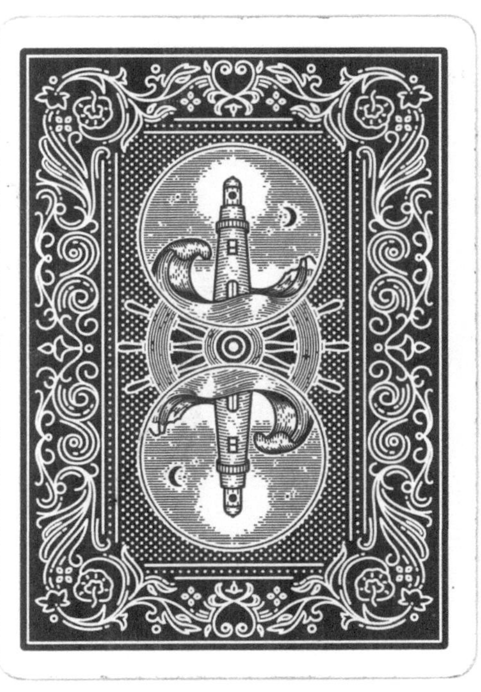

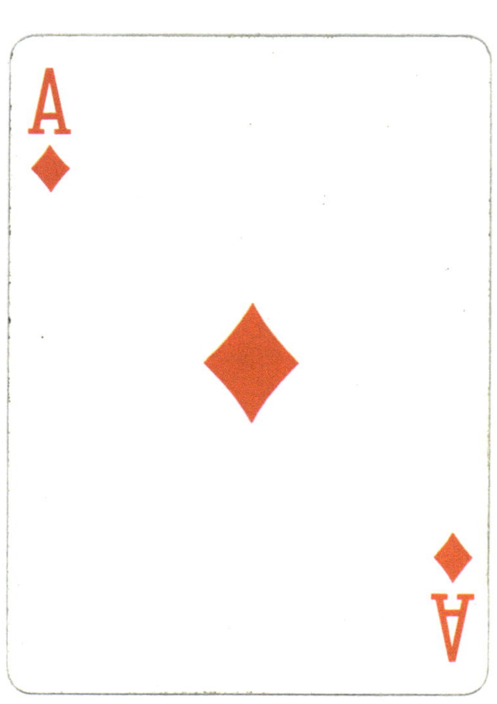

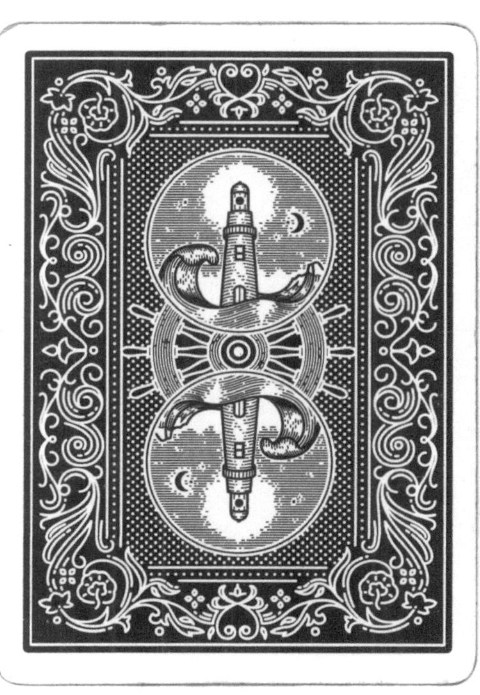

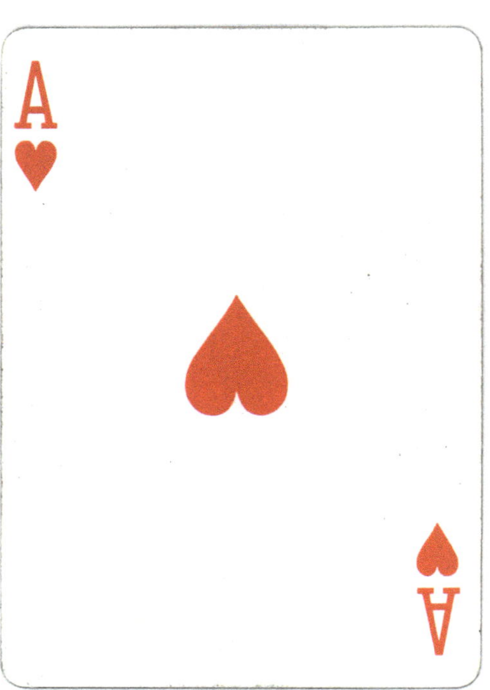

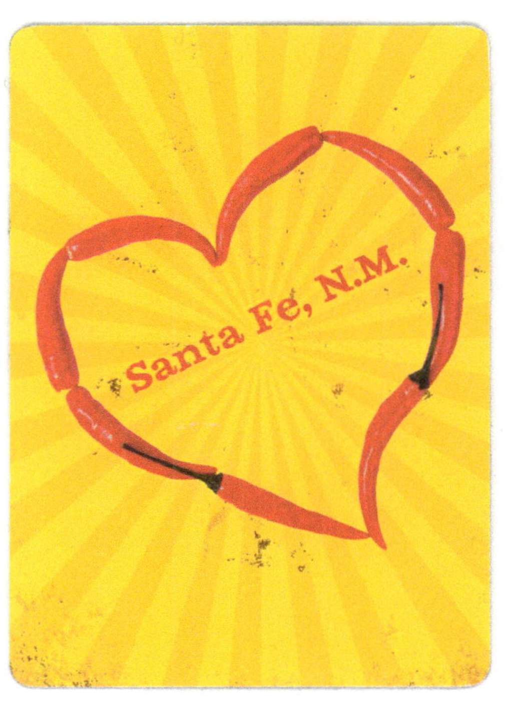

Santa Fe, N.M.

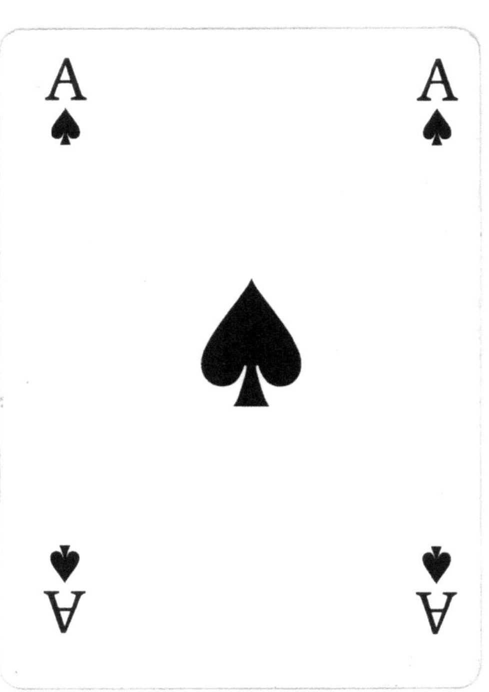

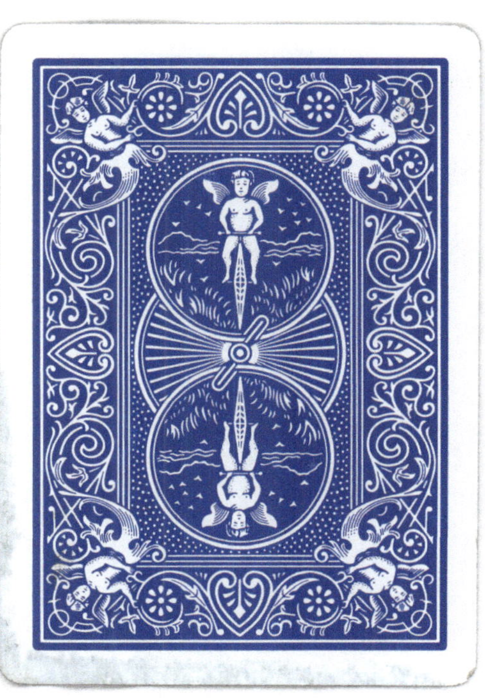

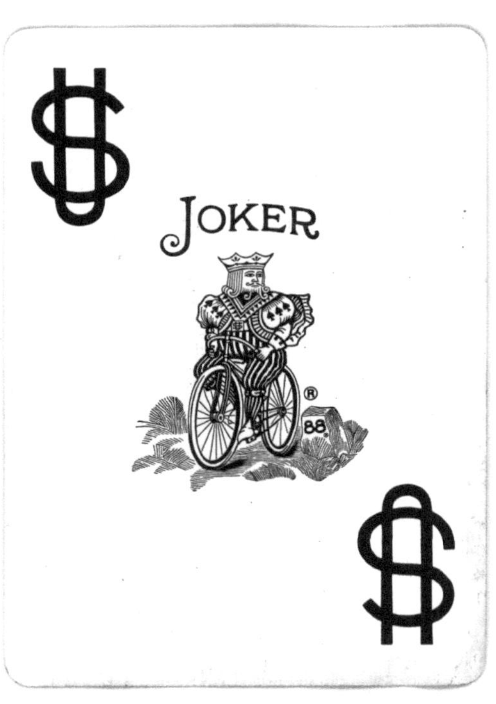

$
JOKER
88.
$

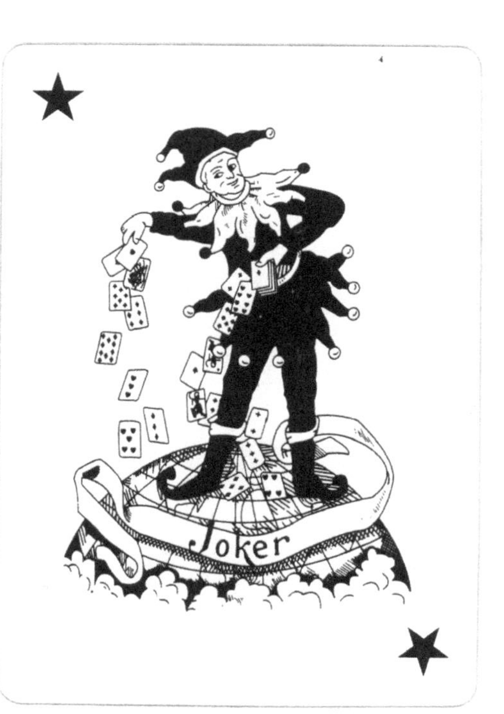

Joker

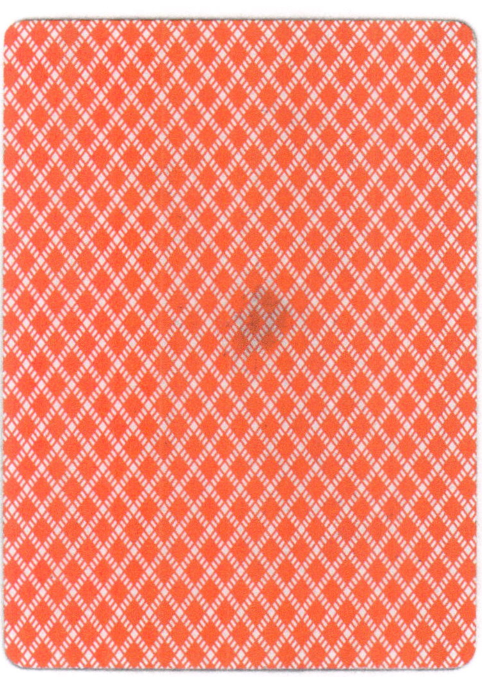

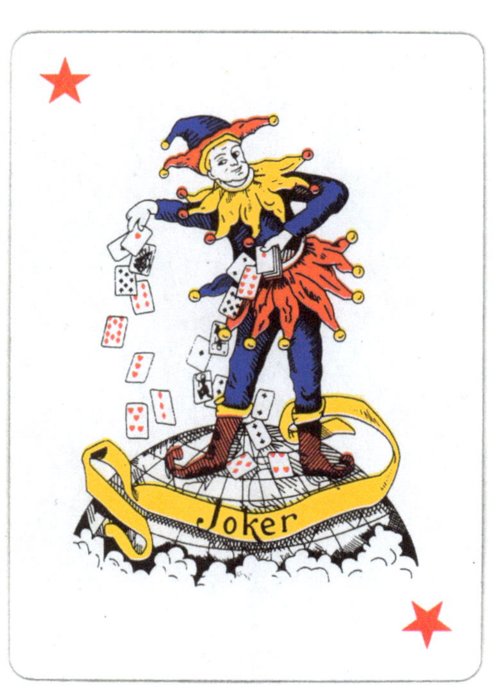

Joker

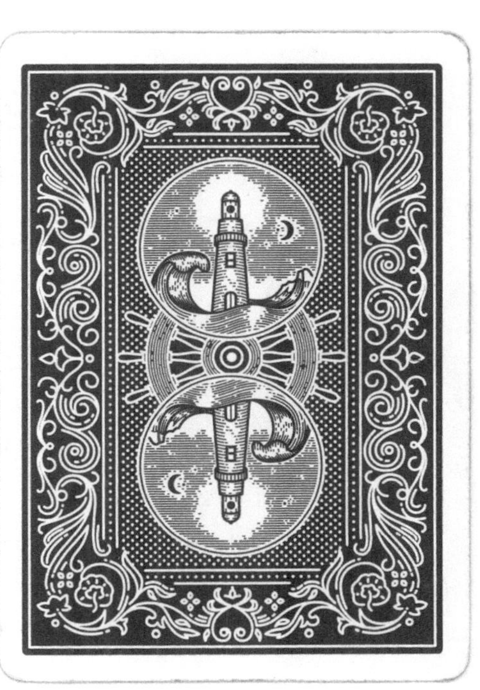

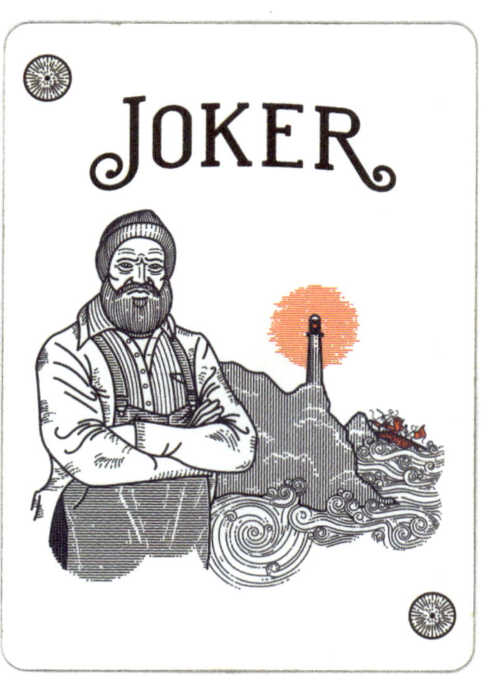
JOKER

www.ingramcontent.com/pod-product-compliance
Lightning Source LLC
Chambersburg PA
CBHW040322240726
48664CB00006B/1602